THE QUICKSILVER YEARS

The Hopes and Fears of Early Adolescence

Peter L. Benson
Dorothy L. Williams
Arthur L. Johnson

1817

Harper & Row, Publishers, San Francisco

Cambridge, Hagerstown, New York, Philadelphia, Washington
London, Mexico City, São Paulo, Singapore, Sydney

To all adults everywhere who teach, guide, plan
for, support, worry over, watch, and love
children who are passing through the
quicksilver years

FIRST EDITION

ISBN 0-86683-535-0

87 88 89 90 91 RRD 10 9 8 7 6 5 4 3 2 1

Contents

PART 1: YOUNG ADOLESCENTS

PART 2: YOUNG ADOLESCENTS AND THEIR FAMILIES

Figures

Tables

Preface

In 1984 an earlier draft of this manuscript reported data on America's young adolescents to the thirteen national youth-serving agencies who had collaborated with Search Institute in conducting a unique and massive survey of a sample of their youth. Each agency also received an individual report focusing on their own population of young adolescents and parents; many of the agencies subsequently made program changes suggested by their own report. Those reports issued to each of the thirteen agencies are their exclusive property, but the composite data, the figures describing all thirteen populations combined, are at the disposal of Search Institute. This book is based on those combined figures.

Word about the original report, four hundred pages long in its typewritten form, began gradually to spread, not only among leadership and volunteers in the thirteen organizations, but also outside their circles. We had apparently touched a responsive chord. Without our having made any systematic effort to publicize it, we have been beseiged with requests for copies of the report. Requests continue to come from public school superintendents, principals, classroom teachers, private schools, state and national legislators, government agencies, organizations related to family life, clergy and church youth workers, foundations, parents, judges, social workers, psychologists, and college professors. What appears to be common to all these is a hunger for up-to-date information on America's young adolescents. Because of this interest, we are pleased that Harper and Row has chosen to publish this book, making the results of our research more accessible to the many who want this information.

This volume owes its life and its shape to a great many persons other than those whose names appear on its cover. First of all, we owe our appreciation to Merton Strommen, founder of Search Institute and author of the proposal for the research project that produced the data. In addition to conceptualizing the project, over a period of months he visited the offices of the national youth-serving agencies to secure their cooperation in the project and participated actively as a member of the research team from start to finish.

We also express our gratitude to The Lilly Endowment of Indianapolis for major funding of the project and particularly to Robert Lynn and Susan Wisely of the Lilly staff, who guided the proposal through the process of examination and final approval.

For the support of the Piton Foundation we are deeply grateful. Unwilling to see the information in this book confined to a research report, the Foundation provided funding that permitted us to rewrite this book, making it accessible to a wider audience.

We also acknowledge the contribution of Lutheran Brotherhood, which generously contributed computer facilities to carry out the analysis of the massive amount of data collected.

We must also thank the thirteen agencies themselves, which allocated funds to carry out part of the survey work within their own constituencies, devoted extensive staff time to advisory committee meetings, travel, and critical review of project reports, and committed themselves from the outset to take seriously the information yielded by the survey.

The contribution of the agency representatives who worked on the project advisory council is enormous. They came together as a group of strangers, most of them never having worked together before, and developed a method of making decisions and carrying out tasks that worked. Their names are given below.

For the African Methodist Episcopal Church
    Edgar Mack
    Kenneth Hill

For the American Lutheran Church
    Kenneth Pohlmann
    Richard Bents

For the Baptist General Conference
    L. Ted Johnson
    Herbert Hage
    Carolyn Olson
    James Parsons
    Robert Samuelson

For the Churches of God, General Conference
    Stephen Dunn
    Wayne L. Heffner

For the Evangelical Covenant Church
   David Noreen
   John Kepler

For the 4-H Extension
   Hope S. Daugherty
   Ronald Daly

For the Lutheran Church—Missouri Synod
   Richard Bimler
   Terry Dittmer

For the National Association of Homes for Children
   Heyward Prince
   Alec Allen
   Arlin Ness

For the National Catholic Education Association
   Bruno Manno

For the Presbyterian Church in the United States
   Dee Koza-Woodward

For the Sunday School Board of the Southern Baptist Convention
   Bob R. Taylor
   J. Clifford Tharp

For the United Church of Christ
   Larry E. Kalp

For the United Methodist Church
   Robert G. Cagle

Central to this book and the project itself, of course, is the contribution of time and thought given by the thousands of young people and their parents who completed the surveys. Their willingness to share what they think, care about, and worry over made the project possible.

On our staff at Search Institute many people have contributed to the work of the project. Shelby Andress and John Forliti have given thought, leadership, and counsel at many points. Carolyn Eklin checked details and edited copy with precision and grace. Jan Mills served as primary word processor, not only for this manuscript and its 1984 predecessor, but for each of the thirteen reports to individual agencies. Jean Wachs worked together with Jan to marshal the arrangements for the national conference to celebrate completion of the 1984 report. Elizabeth Holman, Joe Erickson, Dean Linnell, Bonnie Tracy, and Kathy Howg have all given careful attention to the numbers and words included in this volume. Phillip Wood supervised the computer work and contributed his analytic insights.

Throughout the writing of this book we have been aware of two things: The first is that, whereas in the past, decision makers have had to rely mostly on speculation informed by memory in making decisions about this age group, the availability of this factual data will contribute to more intelligent, more effective decisions and action. The second is that this work only lays the foundation for further study that will enable us to learn still more about these engaging, passionate, and impressionable young people.

March 1986

Peter L. Benson
Dorothy L. Williams
Arthur L. Johnson

Part 1

YOUNG ADOLESCENTS

CHAPTER 1

The Quicksilver Years: Grades Five Through Nine

As their child matures through the elementary grades and approaches sixth or seventh grade, parents grow watchful. At some point between fifth and ninth grade, changes will occur, changes that come with the transition from childhood to adolescence. Parents may experience their child's passage from childhood to adolescence as smooth, gradual, and relatively serene, or they may witness tantrums, tears, and trauma. It's hard to predict the emotional climate that will surround a given child's entry into adolescence.

Predicting the rate at which the transition will occur is equally difficult. Some children enter early adolescence slowly, over an extended period of time; some change almost overnight. But eventually the transition does occur, and the child becomes a bona fide adolescent, attaining the physical growth and adopting the thought patterns, interests, friendship styles, and identity struggles peculiar to teenagers.

The "teenager" period usually lasts from about fifteen to nineteen, and the development and behaviors of this older group of adolescents have been the focus of considerable research. However, until recently, researchers have given little serious attention to the characteristics and behavior of young people in the period of transition from child to teenager—the ten- through fourteen-year-olds who populate the nation's middle schools and junior highs.

One teacher who came to a junior high after years of teaching high school describes the experience like this: "High school students come into the classroom, sit down, and wait for class to start. But when I walk into a junior high classroom, the place bubbles with activity. Kids are sharpening pencils, trying to open windows, rearranging the bulletin board, rummaging for permission slips at my desk, sitting backwards in their seats, tying their shoes, or rushing up to me, declaring with great urgency, 'I gotta go to my locker. I forgot something.' "

Many who work with youth think of early adolescence less in terms of agitation and trouble than in terms of excitement and discovery. They see it as that crucial and challenging time when one begins to catch a glimpse of the emerging adult side by side with the child, when leadership begins to make itself visible, when the capacity for abstract thought develops, and when, perhaps for the first time, a parent or a teacher can hold a conversation with the young person that has the tone of adult-to-adult communication.

The period of fifth through ninth grade is a time of significant growth in the life cycle—growth physically, emotionally, and cognitively. It is not an easy or quiet time—not for youth themselves, nor for their parents, nor for adults who devote their lives to helping young people successfully negotiate the challenges of growing up in a complex world.

In spite of the significance of early adolescence as a major turning point in the life cycle, little research has been made available to help parents, teachers, and others who work with young adolescents deal with them more effectively.

The lack of research information about this age group is curious in view of the fact that, according to Joan Lipsitz, "Early adolescence is a time of growth and change second only to infancy in velocity."[1] As Jerome Kagan wrote a decade ago, "It is a paradox that adolescence should be the period of greatest concern to parents and youth and the era least well comprehended by psychologists. Our understanding of the human infant has been enhanced enormously during the last decade as elegant methodology and rich theory were simultaneously focused on the first year. But no comparable wisdom has been accumulated for early adolescence."[2] This book represents the first major effort to study this mercurial period of life and to chart the patterns and regularities of this seemingly irregular time.

Today's young adolescents are wrestling with information and choices that their parents did not confront until they were in high school, or even later. We now know, from this study as well as others done by Search Institute,[3] that about one fourth of fifth through ninth graders have attended parties where young people of their own age were drinking. About 22 percent of the eighth and ninth graders in this sample report that they were drunk at least once during the year prior to the survey. Not only are these young people being invited to use alcohol and other drugs, but they hear music and see movies that depict and glorify a mix of sexual exploitation and violence.

Adults who work with young people need greater knowledge and more effective tools to combat these negative influences. Their goal, as always, is to ensure that young adolescents emerge from their quicksilver years healthy in body and mind and ready to build on the secure foundation that a caring and supportive early adolescence provides. Yet, providing that foundation is far more difficult today than it used to be.

THE SEARCH INSTITUTE SURVEY

In 1980, Search Institute, with major funding provided by The Lilly Endowment, invited a group of representatives of thirteen youth-serving organizations to join in a national study of this vital age group. (These organizations are listed in Table 1.1.) Each of the agencies agreed to administer a survey prepared by Search Institute to a national, representative sample of their young members or constituents. Through the cooperation of this unique group of agencies, we are now able to make summarizing statements about the thoughts, beliefs, values, and behaviors of young adolescents at each grade level, fifth through ninth, and to compare and contrast those characteristics among boys and girls.

In addition to surveying young people in fifth through ninth grade, we proposed to survey their parents, too. The more cautious among agency representatives warned that the addition of the parent group might be enough added burden to impair or to sink the project. We believed, however, that the inclusion of parents would enable us to explore how their beliefs, values, and behaviors relate to the beliefs, values, and behaviors of their children, yielding a richer fund of information than the study of youth only. That benefit was too attractive to ignore.

Many parents—more than ten thousand of them—accepted the invitation to cooperate in the study. As a result, this book reports what we have discovered about more than eight thousand fifth- through ninth-graders and what we know about their parents, as well. Further, we are able to describe some of the important connections that exist between the characteristics of children and their parents. Knowing more about these connections may give us clues to the prevention of some of the more troubling problems of this transitional age.

Given the rising rate of adolescent suicide and the continuing tragedy of teenage pregnancies and adolescent alcohol and drug use, those who work with young people and their parents—judges, social workers, teachers, school administrators, family therapists, counselors—must understand what factors contribute to the development of these problems and, further, what conditions are most characteristic of the young people who avoid such problems.

Table 1.1 gives the number of young adolescents and parents who participated in the study and the percentage that come from each of the national youth-serving organizations. (See page 6.) One of the first questions we looked at was this: How closely do these samples represent the general population? And then, how accurately can the study report the way life is—fears, worries, concerns, enthusiasms, hopes, and problems—for all young adolescents?

Table 1.1 Sample Sizes and Origins

	Sample Sizes					
Grade in school	Young Adolescents			Parents		
	Boys	Girls	Total	Mothers	Fathers	Total
5th	660	720	1,380			
6th	807	852	1,659			
7th	866	978	1,844			
8th	888	1,010	1,898			
9th	586	677	1,263			
Total	3,807	4,237	8,165*	6,076	4,391	10,467

	Sample Origins		
Sponsoring Agency	Percent of Young Adolescent Sample	Percent of Mother Sample	Percent of Father Sample
African Methodist Episcopal Church	3%	1%	2%
American Lutheran Church	10%	14%	13%
Baptist General Conference	7%	10%	8%
Churches of God, General Conference	4%	5%	5%
Evangelical Covenant Church	6%	8%	7%
4-H Extension	14%	12%	14%
Lutheran Church—Missouri Synod	7%	9%	8%
National Association of Homes for Children	7%	0%	0%
National Catholic Educational Association	14%	8%	10%
Presbyterian Church/U.S.	5%	7%	6%
Southern Baptist Convention	8%	8%	9%
United Church of Christ	8%	9%	9%
United Methodist Church	8%	10%	9%

* Includes 121 young adolescents, grade or sex unknown.

Because ten of the thirteen participating organizations are national Protestant denominations, the study is weighted toward families that maintain some association with a church. The eleventh agency, the National 4-H, is not connected in any way with a church, although the majority of youth and parents in the 4-H sample said they were associated with a local congregation. Many of the residential facilities affiliated with the National Association of Homes for Children are church-related; however, the youth they serve are not necessarily from church-related backgrounds.

The thirteenth organization, the National Catholic Educational Association, contributed 14 percent of the young adolescent sample, 10 percent of the father sample, and 8 percent of the mother sample. All of these youth were enrolled in Catholic elementary schools, and about 90 percent of them claim a Catholic religious affiliation.

The following compares the religious affiliation of the samples and the religious affiliation of the American adult population reported in a recent Gallup poll:[4]

	Survey Sample			Nationally
	Youth	Mothers	Fathers	
Baptist	22%	20%	19%	19%
Lutheran	19%	22%	23%	6%
United Methodist	14%	16%	14%	10%
Presbyterian	7%	7%	8%	4%
Other Protestant	21%	21%	23%	20%
Total Protestant	83%	86%	87%	59%
Roman Catholic	15%	12%	9%	28%
Jewish	<1%	<1%	<1%	2%
Other	<1%	<1%	<1%	4%
None	2%	2%	4%	7%

Compared with national religious preferences, our total sample is more Protestant, less Catholic. Among Protestant groups, Lutherans are overrepresented. However, although the survey samples do not precisely represent, they certainly approximate the national distribution of youth and parents affiliated with Protestant and Catholic congregations or parishes. Since the national figures show that 87 percent of all Americans claim either a Protestant or Catholic religious preference, and that 70 percent report membership in a church,[5] we believe that these data can be taken as representative of a large segment of the population of young adolescents in America, as long as the following cautions are kept in mind:

1. In most congregations, some young adolescents who were selected to participate did so. Others did not. Project funds did not permit an investigation of how participants and nonparticipants differed. The youth sample likely overrepresents young adolescents who are active in the church, and whose parents are also active, and underrepresents less active youth and those with emotional or behavioral problems. The other three agencies, however—National Association of Homes for Children, National Catholic Educational Association, and 4-H—surveyed captive audiences. These three, making up 35 percent of the youth sample, are likely to be more nearly representative of their national constituencies.
2. As shown in Table 1.2, our sample differs from the national population of youth and families in some ways. Our sample overrepresents two groups: the North Central states and parents with four years of college. It underrepresents three groups: Black and Hispanic youth and youth from single-parent families. In most other respects, however, our sample closely approximates the national population.
3. The mothers of about 2,000 adolescents did not respond to the survey. The fathers of about 3,500 also did not respond. Some of these parents may not have responded because they were experiencing family or marital stress. Only a nominal sample of thirty parents whose children are affiliated with the National Association of Homes for Children participated, with the result that the parent samples have a smaller percentage of single parents than of youth who say they live in a single-parent household. For these reasons, the parent sample probably reflects less of the stress and tension found in some families than does the young adolescent sample.

In summary, the findings of this study reflect the responses of youth and parents who are relatively stable, both emotionally and socially, and who are relatively active in a church, and although this study does not cover the entire population, it does provide data about a major segment of young adolescents and their parents.

Table 1.2. **Young Adolescent Sample Compared with 1980 National Census Data**

Characteristic	Young Adolescent Sample	National Census Data
Region[6]		
North East	14%	22%
North Central	39%	26%
South	33%	33%
West	13%	19%
Family Income[7]		
$ 9,999 or less	6%	10%
$10,000–$19,999	18%	16%
$20,000 or more	76%	74%
Race[8]		
Black	7%	15%
Asian	1%	2%
Hispanic	2%	8%
Hometown Population[9]		
Under 5,000	35%	31%
5,000–25,000	20%	19%
25,001–50,000	9%	10%
50,001–100,000	7%	8%
100,001–500,000	15%	13%
500,001 or more	14%	13%
Family		
Lives with two parents	84%	74%
Lives with mother, father absent	11%	21%
Lives with father, mother absent	1%	2%
Lives with neither mother nor father	3%	3%
Mother in Labor Force[10]	59%	55%
Education of Parents[11]		
Mother with 4 years of college or more	38%	13%
Father with 4 years of college or more	43%	22%

A final caution is related to the design of the project. The design we used to gather information on young adolescents is cross-sectional. That means that we present an overview of youth in five different grades, all at one time. Although this allows us to look at differences among youth in different grades, it does not give us precise information on how individuals change between fifth and ninth grade. We are able only to estimate the degree and timing of change by comparing one group of youth who are fifth graders with different groups who are older. Current fifth graders will not grow up in exactly the same social, economic, or historical environment as current ninth graders, so we need to exercise some caution in drawing firm conclusions about the path, timing, and sequence of development during early adolescence. But we can also say that we know, with reasonable certainty, some important new things about this fascinating age group—the ten- to fourteen-year-olds—who trouble and enliven the world of the many adults who guide, plan for, support, worry over, admonish, watch, fear for, and love them.

MAJOR FINDINGS

Countless hours of survey-taking time were invested in this project, almost twenty thousand surveys were processed, many hours of computer time were used, and hundreds of hours of analysis were completed by a team of people who studied the enormous stacks of printouts. As the result of this huge expenditure of time and care, what have we learned? This book chronicles findings in a wide range of areas. Here are some of the significant themes readers will find:

At first glance, what we see about young adolescents is their chaotic activity and their tendency to want to be treated as adults but to act like children. Nevertheless, hidden under the chaos are real signs of growth, of creative adaptation to a profusion of internal and external changes. It is a wonder, in some ways, that youth survive the simultaneous onslaught of biological, emotional, and cognitive changes. Yet, when we take a single snapshot of this active group, we see the vast majority doing constructive things like building friendship skills, growing in empathy, valuing parents and family, struggling with issues of freedom and independence, opposing racial discrimination, caring about the hungry and poor, and contemplating the future.

However, even though we find many young adolescents and parents on relatively solid ground, concerns and problems are also visible. Many of them constitute a real threat to healthy development. Among these are experimentation with sexual intercourse, as reported by 20 percent of seventh, eighth, and ninth grade students; worry about sexual and physical abuse expressed by a significant number of young adolescents; the evidence of abuse by some young adolescents of alcohol and other mood-altering chemicals; worry about the possibility of nuclear destruction; the relatively frequent occurrence of certain forms of aggression among some young adolescents; and the social alienation experienced by some youth, particularly boys.

We find that young people entering adolescence, in spite of a veneer of sophistication, are still as uncertain about their own identity, as eager for a loosening of parental restraints, as interested in their friends, and as idealistic as their parents remember being. Granted, there are problems—those just mentioned as well as others. Yet, in spite of the too-well-advertised generation gap, we find that a great many of these youngsters, even the oldest of them, are more likely to turn to their parents when worried or in trouble than to their peers.

We find some good news for families from this study, too. In recent years we have become accustomed to hearing that American families are in serious trouble. According to the mass media, marriages are disintegrating in epidemic numbers, parents and children spend little time with each other, children are raised by their peers rather than their parents, and many children are being victimized by rejecting or abusing adults.

The picture that emerges from our data is quite different. We do not deny that divorce and separation have touched many households, that parents sometimes find themselves stretched thin over conflicting responsibilities to job, community, and family, and that some children live in chaotic and violent homes. But, side by side with that, we also see parents genuinely struggling to be good parents. We see young adolescents who feel relatively good about their parents and enjoy spending time with them. We observe parent-child relationships that have much more affection and support in them than rejection or hostility.

Not all youth and families in our study are functioning in total harmony, of course. These families have their own stresses and problems. However, we find that the needs, despairs, and longings of youth and parents tend to be more subtle, less catastrophic, and perhaps more benign than commonly depicted. And this provides, for most young adolescents, a positive setting and a strong foundation for growth toward productive and satisfying lives.

In the midst of the young adolescent period, parents are often struck with self-doubt. Is it all worth anything? Is anything I'm saying getting through? Should I insist on what I think is right, or am I simply wasting my breath? Our data are quite clear at this point. In the majority of cases, what parents say and do is important, and the example they set is even more significant. Both the parental modeling and the family atmosphere have measurable impact on what young adolescents value, believe, and do.

CHAPTER 2

Social Context:
School, Mass Media, Church, Peers

· For both boys and girls, school climate becomes less positive with each increment in grade.
· The number of young adolescents who perceive classmates using alcohol and marijuana at school doubles between eighth and ninth grade.
· Half of all young adolescents in this study watch television three hours or more on the average school day.
· Girls have more positive attitudes toward the church than boys, but for both boys and girls, attitudes toward the church become less favorable between the fifth and ninth grade.
· Between fifth and ninth grade, peer influence increases and parent influence decreases. However, in no grade does peer influence outweigh the influence of parents.

Young adolescents spend a major part of their lives outside the direct influence of parents. In most cases the time spent away from parents increases gradually between the ages of ten and fourteen as children are drawn into a variety of structured events—organized athletic activities, school clubs and organizations, church youth programs, and the activities of other youth-serving organizations.

Moreover, some young adolescents spend a good deal of time just "hanging out." Enjoying greater freedom than they had in childhood, they begin to spend more free time moving about the neighborhood and community. In these contexts, the young adolescent interacts with peers and friends more often than with adults.

The young adolescent's world expands. In this expanding world, many social or environmental factors bear on how he or she will develop. This chapter looks at young adolescents' experiences with four of these factors: school, mass media, church, and peers. Later chapters examine a fifth factor—the family.

SCHOOL

School is a given in the lives of North American children. A relatively modern social invention, school was designed to mold and nurture both mind and character. How do young people feel about school? What kind of school climate do they experience?

INTEREST IN SCHOOL

People in the field of education often note the anticipation and excitement with which most children enter kindergarten or first grade and the distaste for school that many of these same children exhibit after ten or twelve years in the school environment. What happens, they wonder, that causes that excitement and anticipation to drain away? And when does it happen?

We do not propose to answer the first question, but we can demonstrate the curve of interest in our sample of students between fifth and ninth grade. Three items on our survey reveal their feelings about school. Here are the items and the student responses:

	5th	6th	7th	8th	9th
My teachers care a lot about me.					
Percent who answer "often true" or "very often true"	52	48	38	38	30
How interesting to you are your courses at school?					
Percent who think most are interesting or exciting	49	43	39	31	39
How do you feel about going to school?					
Percent who like school "very much" or "quite a bit"	57	52	50	51	55

The perception of teachers as caring decreases quite significantly across the five grades. The sizable drop between sixth and seventh grade is probably due, in part, to the fact that many students experience a change from one teacher in grade school to many teachers in a junior high setting.[1] The percentages for the other two items also decrease, but rise again in ninth grade.

Attitudes toward school are similar for boys and girls on some questions and different on others. At all grade levels girls are more interested in school than boys, but when interest in school declines in certain grades it does so for both boys and girls. (See Figure 1.) In spite of the decline, however, half or more of the young adolescents in each grade report positive feelings about going to school.

RELATIONSHIP OF INTEREST IN SCHOOL TO OTHER CHARACTERISTICS

When comparing interest in school with other findings, we note some important tendencies. They include the following:[2]

· Young adolescents in public, private, and parochial schools do not differ in their degree of interest in school.
· Young adolescents who have higher interest in school, when compared to those with lower interest, tend to have higher achievement motivation, higher self-esteem, and lower conflict with parents. (See Chapter 3.)
· Interest in school is higher for young adolescents when their perception of the school climate is positive.
· The greater the interest in school, the less young adolescents engage in drug use or antisocial behavior. (See Chapters 10 and 11.)

HOMEWORK

Only a minority of young adolescents do six hours or more of homework each week, as the figures below show, though their numbers increase between fifth and ninth grade. At each of the five grade levels, girls, on the average, report doing more homework than boys.

	5th	6th	7th	8th	9th
In an average week, about how many hours do you spend doing homework?					
Percent who spend 2 hours or less	65	52	39	34	33
Percent who spend 3–5 hours	21	29	33	35	33
Percent who spend 6 hours or more	14	19	28	31	34

PERCEPTIONS OF SCHOOL CLIMATE

Six items in the survey probed students' perceptions of the school environment. The items are of two types: (1) perceptions of the degree to which their classmates show positive attitudes toward school and (2) perceptions of the degree to which they observe problem behaviors (behaviors that interfere with the educational process) at school.

Figure 1 Sex Differences in Attitudes Toward School

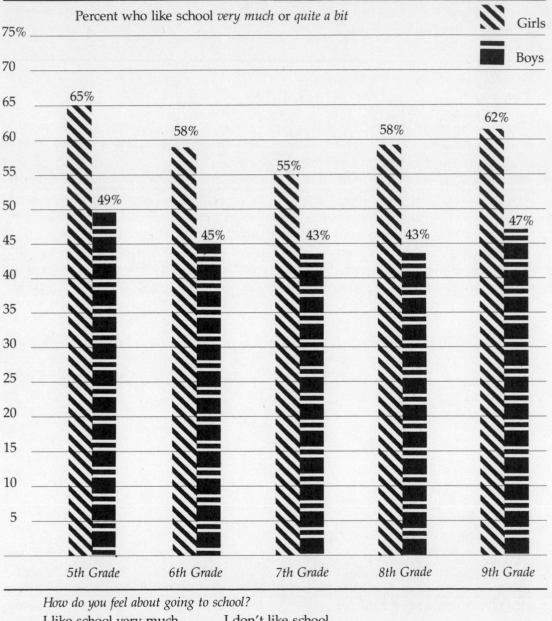

Percent who like school *very much* or *quite a bit*

How do you feel about going to school?

I like school very much   I don't like school
I like school quite a bit   I hate school
I like school some

Young adolescents report the following positive perceptions of their school:

	5th	6th	7th	8th	9th
How much do these things go on at your school?					
Kids feeling good about school					
Percent who answer "very much" or "quite a bit"	38	34	24	22	21
Kids trying to do their best					
Percent who answer "very much" or "quite a bit"	62	54	46	44	39

Note the steady decline on both items across the five grades. The largest shift on both items is between the sixth and seventh grades. A particularly dramatic drop occurs between the fifth and ninth grades in perception of peers' academic motivation.

Consistent with this perceived decrease in a favorable school environment, young adolescents also show increased awareness, between fifth and ninth grade, of problem behaviors occurring at school. With each shift in grade, young adolescents report a rise in each of these four problem behaviors. The most dramatic shift is in the use of alcohol and marijuana perceived between eighth and ninth grades.

	5th	6th	7th	8th	9th
How much do these things go on at your school?					
Kids smoking marijuana (pot, grass)					
Percent who answer "very much" or "quite a bit"	6	7	11	16	34
Kids goofing off in the classroom					
Percent who answer "very much" or "quite a bit"	50	55	64	69	69
Kids drinking alcohol					
Percent who answer "very much" or "quite a bit"	8	7	13	20	38
Kids stealing things					
Percent who answer "very much" or "quite a bit"	14	16	22	21	24

Here is an index of school climate that contains the average rating of the six items listed above. A rating of five would be considered the most positive perception.

	5th	*6th*	*7th*	*8th*	*9th*
Boys	3.68	3.54	3.32	3.17	2.92
Girls	3.75	3.60	3.32	3.22	2.89

Both boys and girls view their school climate less positively with each succeeding grade.[3] Positive perceptions decrease most rapidly between sixth and seventh grade and between eighth and ninth grade. For many young adolescents, these transition points coincide with movement out of one school and into another. We find, in comparing their data, that parochial school students tend to perceive a more positive school climate than students in public schools. We also find, through making other comparisons, that the more one perceives school climate as positive, the less likely one is to engage in antisocial behaviors like fighting or cheating; likewise, the more one perceives school climate as positive, the less likely one is to use drugs or alcohol.[4]

MASS MEDIA

AMOUNT OF MEDIA EXPOSURE

Nearly all young adolescents are exposed to three major forms of mass media. All these forms—television, movies, and rock music—have been a part of the culture for some time. A fourth form included in the survey, videogames, has a much shorter history and already appears to be diminishing in popularity, although at the time of the survey 24 percent of young adolescents spent three hours or more per week playing videogames, a frequency that approaches the figures for television and rock music listed here.

	5th	6th	7th	8th	9th	Total
Hours per school day spent watching television						
Percent who watch 3–4 hours	27	32	30	34	30	31
Percent who watch 5 hours or more	24	22	20	18	18	20
Percent who watch 3 hours or more (sum of the above)	51	54	50	52	47	51
Frequency of going out to see a movie						
Percent who go 1–3 times a month	28	30	35	35	36	33
Percent who go once a week or more	8	8	7	8	10	9
Hours per day spent listening to "hard rock" music						
Percent who listen 2 hours or more	22	23	30	37	41	30

From the above we see that

- Half of all young adolescents in this study spend three hours or more each day watching television.
- Rock music is the only form for which exposure increases with grade in school. (Exposure to television and movies remains relatively stable between fifth and ninth grade.)
- The average young adolescent is exposed to the mass media a total of about four hours per day. Only sleeping and attending school occupy more time.

Boys and girls do not differ in the amount of time spent watching television, or in the frequency of attending movies. However, boys spend more time than girls listening to rock music and playing videogames.[5]

IMPACT OF MEDIA EXPOSURE

Many social science researchers have explored the relationship of television viewing to various forms of aggression.[6] Because acts of violence and aggression are commonplace on television, we need to discover whether exposure to aggression in media breeds acts of aggression among viewers. Contrary to the findings of other research, we found no relationship between television viewing and aggression in our sample. Young adolescents exposed to large amounts of television programming were no more likely to report aggressive actions than those exposed to little or none.

When we look at the impact of videogames, the picture is different. Because of the recency of the videogame phenomenon, little systematic research is available on its impact. Our data, however, reveal a very strong relationship between amount of videogame playing and aggression (including self-reports on vandalism and fighting).[7] Interpreting this finding is difficult. Because many popular videogames are games of aggression in which winning (or scoring points) depends on acts of destruction, a connection between this form of entertainment and aggressive behavior is possible. Videogame playing may encourage aggression. Perhaps young adolescents who engage in aggressive acts are particularly attracted to videogames. The passage of time and further research may contribute greater clarity on this point.

ATTRACTION TO MEDIA SEX AND VIOLENCE

Young adolescents were asked these two questions about their attraction to "R" and "X" rated movies and media violence.

	5th	6th	7th	8th	9th
How much do you like to see movies that are "R" or "X" rated?					
Percent who answer "very much" or "quite a bit"					
Boys	28	31	37	50	51
Girls	17	20	24	30	30
How much do you like to see movies that show people getting hurt or killed?					
Percent who answer "very much" or "quite a bit"					
Boys	30	28	31	35	35
Girls	9	12	11	11	12

We do not know exactly what young adolescents think "R" and "X" rated means in terms of sexual content, nor do we know what actual contact young adolescents have had with "R" or "X" rated movies. It is likely that they understand these kinds of movies to have more explicit sexual content than they are exposed to in "G" and "PG" movies, and the more restricted media forms may seem more attractive because they are restricted. The rating "for mature viewers only" no doubt serves as a kind of enticement.

Although both sexes show increased interest in "R" and "X" movies, not surprisingly, the increase is more dramatic for boys than for girls. Other research has pointed out that boys and girls evolve differently into sexual activity.[8] For girls, sexual arousal is more likely to occur in a relational context. "The onset of sexual activity for girls involves incorporating it into social roles and an identity wherein capacities for tenderness, self-disclosure, and intimacy are already present. For the boy, on the other hand, the pathway to mature heterosexual behavior is far more likely to involve sexuality first, and only secondarily the capacity for loving relationships."[9] Accordingly, boys are more attracted than girls to erotic stimuli. What is noteworthy in our data is the finding that differences between boys and girls occur as early as the fifth grade and continue through each of the years up to the ninth grade.

The differences between the sexes in attraction to media violence is even more pronounced. Part of this difference is likely due to different socialization experiences in which boys, more than girls, receive modeling, rewards, and encouragement for aggressive action and aggressive ways of resolving conflict.

CHURCH

Religious institutions provide an important social context for young adolescents. Connection with a religious institution, whether church or synagogue, is a reality for the vast majority of fifth- through ninth-grade youth. Most parents apparently still consider church or synagogue to be an important socializing agent, so they encourage or require their children to attend.

Even though most young adolescents are church affiliated, relatively little is known about what role that connection plays in their lives.[10] In part, this lack of knowledge is due to the fact that social scientists have paid very little attention to early adolescence. The vacuum also reflects a prevailing tendency—most strongly seen in psychology but present in other disciplines as well—to ignore the religious dimension (including church affiliation) in human experience.

CHURCH ATTENDANCE

With this population of young adolescents, we would expect church attendance rates to be relatively high and relatively stable across grades. The following figures confirm that expectation. The rates of attendance for once a week or more are relatively high and stable. Rates are highest for seventh and eighth grade, which might reflect requirements of religious instruction programs (such as pre-confirmation study) often occurring during these two years. Note the decline in the weekly attendance of ninth-grade boys. This change fits a common theme throughout this report: a number of significant changes seem to occur for boys between the eighth and ninth grades.

	5th	6th	7th	8th	9th	Total
How often do you attend worship services at a church or synagogue?						
Percent who never attend						
Boys	4	3	4	3	6	4
Girls	3	3	3	2	3	3
Percent who attend several times a year						
Boys	10	7	5	5	9	7
Girls	11	9	6	5	5	7
Percent who attend about once a month						
Boys	3	4	4	4	4	4
Girls	4	3	2	3	4	3
Percent who attend 2–3 times a month						
Boys	13	19	15	16	18	16
Girls	14	14	15	13	16	14
Percent who attend once a week or more						
Boys	69	68	72	72	64	69
Girls	67	71	75	78	72	73

ATTITUDES TOWARD THE CHURCH

Attendance rates do not reveal much about how young adolescents feel about the church. In all probability, young adolescents do not have complete freedom to decide whether or not to attend religious services; parental expectations still carry considerable weight during this age period. However, we can expect attitudes and perceptions about church to tell us more. Three survey items probed these dimensions, and responses to them are listed here:

	5th	6th	7th	8th	9th
How important is your church or synagogue to you?					
Percent who answer "very" or "extremely" important					
Boys	54	49	45	42	40
Girls	58	53	49	48	51
Total	56	51	47	45	46

	5th	6th	7th	8th	9th

How much does your church or synagogue
help you answer important questions you have
about life?
  Percent who answer "very much" or "quite
  a bit"

	5th	6th	7th	8th	9th
Boys	42	41	37	37	34
Girls	46	44	43	39	42
Total	44	43	40	38	38

Of the things you want most in life, how much
do you want to be part of a church or
synagogue?
  Percent who answer "very much" or "at the
  top of the list"

	5th	6th	7th	8th	9th
Boys	57	56	51	49	48
Girls	62	61	57	51	58
Total	60	59	54	50	53

Three important patterns appear in these findings:

· Girls across the five grades hold more positive attitudes toward the church than do boys.
· For both boys and girls, attitudes toward the church become somewhat less favorable with advances in grade.
· The decline in favorable attitudes is more pronounced among boys.

These changes are not dramatic. Nonetheless, the changes do suggest a trend in which attitudes toward the institutional church become less favorable between fifth and ninth grade. The period from seventh to ninth grade may be the time, particularly for boys, when youth first begin to reflect on or evaluate the church. This is the age when some young people are first able to contemplate how things could be and, consequently, to fathom the gap that exists between what *is* and what *could be*. When young people begin using abstract reasoning processes, they often are initially critical of institutions such as school, family, and church that they formerly took for granted.

RELATIONSHIP OF POSITIVE ATTITUDES TOWARD THE CHURCH AND OTHER
FACTORS

Young adolescents with strongly positive attitudes toward the church are distinguished primarily by a set of factors involving parents' religious behavior.

Compared with those who have less favorable attitudes to the church, young adolescents with more favorable attitudes are more likely to have mothers and fathers who consider religion important and a home environment in which religion is expressed and talked about.[11]

Detractors commonly voice three reasons why they believe church involvement for youth is not always desirable: that church activity functions mainly to inhibit youth, that churches fail to show the kind of compassion for people they stand for, and that churches mold young adolescents to adopt prevailing cultural attitudes, including racial prejudice.

Our data do not support these assertions.[12] Instead, we find that positive attitudes toward church are related to less use of drugs and alcohol, less anti-social behavior, and more concern for others. Nor are positive attitudes toward church related to racial prejudice—either positively or negatively. Another form of prejudice—ageism—is in fact lower when positive attitudes toward church are high.

INVOLVEMENT IN CHURCH YOUTH PROGRAMS

Young adolescents in the project were asked how much they participate in a church-related youth program (excluding religious instruction such as Sunday School). Their responses follow:

	5th	6th	7th	8th	9th
Percent having no youth program at their church or synagogue					
Boys	24	28	20	16	6
Girls	32	28	16	15	8
Percent who "never go"					
Boys	18	17	16	17	18
Girls	16	10	13	13	11
Percent who go "once in a while" or "sometimes"					
Boys	24	24	26	29	31
Girls	20	26	23	24	28
Percent who go "often"					
Boys	35	31	38	39	45
Girls	32	36	48	48	54

Girls are more active than boys in church youth programs, particularly in the seventh- to ninth-grade period. This fits a general pattern of more church activity among girls than boys.

FRIENDS AND PEERS

Children live in two worlds—one of parents and one of peers. As they grow older, friends and peers take on increasing importance. As shown in Figure 2, young adolescents increasingly find more enjoyment in the company of peers than of parents. Social scientists tell us that this friend and peer network is absolutely essential for healthy development. Through the trial and error of peer relationships children and adolescents learn much about sex roles, values, morality, and the expression and control of aggression.

Here we look at four aspects of friends and peers during early adolescence: concern about friendship, the composition of the friendship network, peer versus parent influence, and the consequences of peer relationships.

CONCERN ABOUT FRIENDSHIP

To what extent are young adolescents concerned about friendship? As will be shown in Chapter 4, although friends are an important dimension in the lives of fifth- through ninth-graders, they are not the primary concern. Other factors, such as school achievement and the quality of family life, are equal to, or above, friendship in importance to young adolescents. This project tells us two other important things about young adolescents' friendship concerns: (1) concern about friendship stays fairly constant throughout the period of fifth through ninth grade, neither rising nor falling in any significant fashion across these five years and (2) at each grade in the fifth- through ninth-grade period, concern about friendship is higher for girls than for boys.

THE FRIENDSHIP NETWORK

As the following figures show, there are two changes in friendship circles during the years of early adolescence: (1) A dramatic shift to sex integration in friendship circles, the percentage of opposite-sex friends rising with each advance in grade, and (2) A modest shift to greater racial segregation in friendship circles, with ninth-graders reporting more racial segregation than fifth graders.[13]

	5th	6th	7th	8th	9th
How many of your best friends are members of the opposite sex?					
Percent having none	24	19	14	9	7
Percent with half or more	31	37	43	50	57

Figure 2   Sources of Enjoyment: Peers vs. Parents

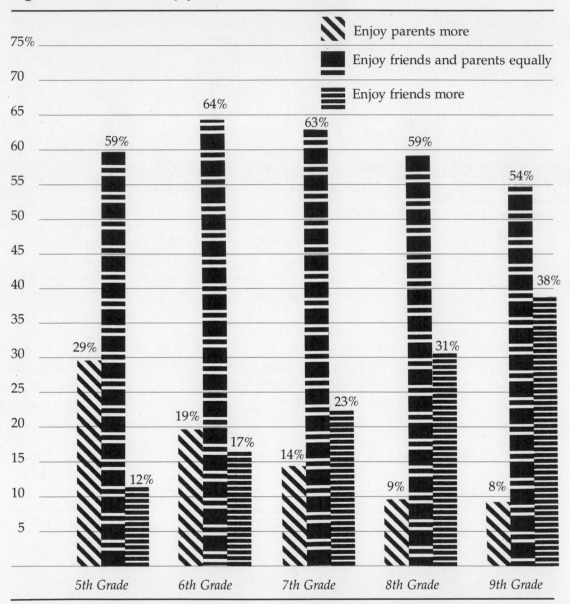

Whom do you enjoy being with more
—your friends or parents?

Parents—I enjoy my parents more
Both—I enjoy my parents and friends equally
Friends—I enjoy my friends more

	5th	6th	7th	8th	9th
How many of your closest friends are of the same race as you?					
Percent with "most" or "all"	74	78	79	82	85

Boys and girls do not differ significantly in the number of sex-integrated friendships. However, girls report greater racial segregation in friendship circles than do boys.

PEER VERSUS PARENT INFLUENCE

A major tenet in the literature on psychological development is that the influence of peers rises and the influence of parents declines during the adolescent years. To date, it has not been clear when this transition begins and "when the influential impact of peers begins to outweigh that of parents."[14]

All three groups in this study—young adolescents, mothers, and fathers— were asked about the relative influence of peers and parents. Figure 3 shows how young adolescents responded when asked from whom they would seek advice.

The changes across the grades are clear. With each succeeding grade in school, the influence of peers increases and the influence of parents decreases. Note, however, that in no grade is peer influence greater than parents'. Had this study extended to tenth grade, we might have seen the relative influence of peers outweighing that of parents.

Mothers and fathers corroborate the patterning reported in Figure 2, as these figures show.

	5th	6th	7th	8th	9th
Asked of mothers:					
Overall, to whom does your child turn when he or she has a problem—parents or peers?					
Percent who answer "parents more"	92	88	83	77	71
Percent who answer "parents and peers equally"	7	10	15	18	21
Percent who answer "peers more"	1	2	2	5	8

Figure 3   Sources of Advice: Peers vs. Parents

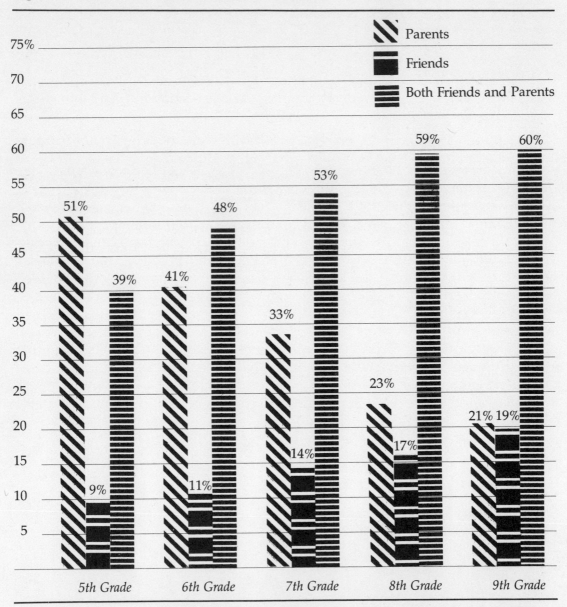

If you had a very important decision to make, to whom would you turn for advice—your friends or parents?

	5th	6th	7th	8th	9th
Asked of fathers:					
Overall, to whom does your child turn when he or she has a problem—parents or peers?					
Percent who answer "parents more"	91	89	84	83	79
Percent who answer "parents and peers equally"	8	10	13	14	17
Percent who answer "peers more"	1	1	3	3	4

As before, peer influence increases with each grade, though parents attribute far less overall influence to peers than do young adolescents.

Six other items in the youth survey speak to the question of peer influence. Young adolescents were presented with a list of six situations and for each were asked whom they would most likely turn to for advice or help: parents, a friend, an adult friend, a relative, a member of the clergy, a teacher or school counselor, or nobody. On all six topics, more young adolescents chose parents than peers, as the numbers below indicate.

	5th	6th	7th	8th	9th
When having trouble in school, I would turn to . . .					
Percent who answer "parent"	54	56	55	48	41
Percent who answer "peer"	11	13	17	22	25
When wondering how to handle my feelings, I would turn to . . .					
Percent who answer "parent"	58	56	47	42	36
Percent who answer "peer"	12	18	24	30	32
When some of my friends start using drugs or alcohol, I would turn to . . .					
Percent who answer "parent"	45	46	41	35	31
Percent who answer "peer"	9	9	10	9	10
When having questions about sex, I would turn to . . .					
Percent who answer "parent"	57	57	51	46	38
Percent who answer "peer"	13	15	19	24	28
When feeling guilty about something I have done, I would turn to . . .					
Percent who answer "parent"	47	43	39	34	29
Percent who answer "peer"	15	21	25	30	35

	5th	6th	7th	8th	9th
When deciding what to do with my life, I would turn to . . .					
Percent who answer "parent"	61	62	64	65	62
Percent who answer "peer"	7	8	8	8	8

Ninth graders selected one situation, "When I feel guilty about something," as the one case in which they would more often seek the advice of a peer. In all other cases, more influence is attributed to parents than peers. For major choices, such as, "When deciding what to do with my life," well over half of young adolescents would seek parental advice.

These data make clear that three dynamics occur between the fifth and ninth grades: peer influence increases, parent influence decreases, and, even though parent influence declines during the period of early adolescence, parents remain the *stronger* of the two influences. However, the degree to which parents are viewed as valuable advice-givers may be affected by the sample of families surveyed. In this study, the sample of young adolescents may be skewed to those with good relationships with parents. If so, these data might overestimate the degree of parent influence on young adolescents in general.

Our data also show that (1) peer influence increases with grade; (2) boys and girls are similar in degree of peer influence in the fifth and sixth grades; but (3) girls in the seventh, eighth, and ninth grades are much more likely than boys to be affected by peer influence.[15]

CONSEQUENCES OF PEER RELATIONSHIPS

Peer influence is a two-edged sword. Peers have a powerful impact on each other, but the influence can be either positive or negative, depending on what attitudes and behaviors are modeled. By and large, the young adolescents in this project do not report a great deal of pressure toward negative behavior from friends, as the responses to the following statement suggest.

	5th	6th	7th	8th	9th
My friends try to get me to do things I believe are wrong.					
Percent who respond "often" or "very often"	15	12	11	9	8

When we combine three items (My friends get into a lot of trouble at school;

I worry that my friends will get me in trouble; My friends try to get me to do things I believe are wrong) to create an index of negative peer pressure, two important findings emerge.[16] Reports of negative peer pressure decline with grade, and boys at each of the five grades report higher levels of negative peer pressure than do girls.

SUMMARY

A number of significant changes occur in young people's relationship to their social environment as they enter early adolescence. These changes are summarized below.

These *decrease* from grade five to grade nine for both boys and girls:
> Interest in school
> Perception of positive school climate
> Positive attitude toward church
> Parent influence

These *increase* from grade five to grade nine for both boys and girls:
> Listening to hard rock music
> Interest in "R" and "X" rated movies
> Number of opposite-sex friends
> Peer influence

Boys more typically than girls experience negative peer pressure and have higher interest in:
> Media violence
> Videogame playing
> Hard rock music
> Sex

Girls more typically than boys demonstrate:
> Higher interest in school
> Greater numbers of hours spent doing homework
> Positive attitude toward the church
> Activity in church youth programs
> Greater peer influence in grades seven, eight, and nine

Between the fifth and ninth grades, young adolescents begin the process of disengaging from major institutional forces such as school and church. At the same time, they begin to discover a wider world that subjects them to new pressures and challenges, often including transitions to new school settings. They develop acquaintance with school peers who engage in a wider range of behaviors, including some behaviors of which most adults disapprove. They begin to build friendship networks in which opposite-sex relationships take on new prominence and significance. Added complexity arises from the major changes that are occurring in their bodies and their ways of thinking.

As the protective authority of school, church, and parents begins to subside and the stresses and challenges of a wider world begin to emerge, it is no wonder that young adolescents begin to cling to each other. Networks of friendship become essential for advice on how to cope. And in these peer relationships, young adolescents help each other develop life-shaping values and perspectives. This process is necessary. Although the process neither begins nor ends in early adolescence, early adolescence is one of its pivotal periods.

During early adolescence, youth find themselves in two worlds. One foot is planted in the structured and somewhat controlling world of social institutions, including family, and the other foot is stepping into the larger world. At times, young adolescents want to dive headlong into the larger world, but they need to know that they can always come back to the familiar security of home base. The role of parents, school, and church is particularly crucial through the years of early adolescence. All of these agents should strive to remain benevolent, welcoming, and supportive. Though they may sense a lessening power, their presence and their insistence on maintaining their accustomed roles and functions provide the stability that young adolescents so much need.

Two other related themes emerge in this chapter. One is that the ability of the school to play a gyroscope or stabilizing function is threatened in the transition between grades six and seven and grades eight and nine. Educators and parents must continue to consider how the school can best fill that stabilizing function while meeting the other rapidly changing needs of young adolescents.[17] The second theme has to do with trends in the data on boys. Young adolescent boys report both greater disengagement from school and church than do girls and greater negative peer pressure. This combination may require schools, churches, other youth-serving agencies, and parents to expend additional energy in finding ways to help boys cope with these challenges of early adolescence.

CHAPTER 3

Development: Autonomy, Social Competence, Identity, Achievement, Sexuality

- Boys and girls experience similar gains in autonomy between fifth and ninth grade.
- Only a small minority of young adolescents report major conflicts with parents.
- Both boys and girls increase in self-disclosure, empathy, and friendship-making skills between the fifth and ninth grade. In all three areas, girls report more competency than boys.
- Social alienation is highest for fifth graders and is higher for boys than for girls.
- Between the fifth and ninth grades, girls develop a less favorable concept of their own body image.
- At each grade level, girls report higher achievement motivation than boys.
- Thirty-nine percent of fifth graders report "being in love." The percentage rises to 51 percent by ninth grade.
- One in five ninth graders report that they have had sexual intercourse. The rate for boys is more than double the rate for girls.
- Only about one third of young adolescents report that they have had "good talks with my parents about sex."

The varieties of growth that occur in young adolescents do not all get equal billing; physical growth, by its very visibility, claims the lion's share of public attention. "My! Haven't you grown!" "Look at those sleeves—too short already and we just bought that jacket last month!" Though physical evidence of growth draws the most frequent comment, growth in other realms also takes place during early adolescence, and this growth, in most cases, will have far greater influence over the young person's total life span than will the physical growth that at this age occasions so much comment.

In this chapter we look at development in five areas: autonomy, social competence, sexuality, identity, and achievement. These five developmental processes neither begin nor end in the age period between ten and fifteen. They are continuous, with development beginning in childhood and proceeding for years after. Our task is to describe how typical growth occurs during early adolescence, realizing that great individual variety exists in the rate at which it occurs.

Although many theorists speculate about the young adolescent's journey through these five areas, little information exists as to the degree and timing of developmental change.[1] This study provides an opportunity to chart broad-stroke changes and to note how these changes differ for boys and girls.

COGNITIVE DEVELOPMENT

As a context for understanding development, we will discuss briefly some of the cognitive developments in early adolescence.[2] One is the gradual development of abstract reasoning processes, frequently called formal operations. This development involves the following five changes:[3]

1. In contrast to childhood thinking, with its sensible here-and-now emphasis, adolescent thinking is associated with the world of *possibilities*. With an ever-increasing ability to use abstractions, the adolescent can distinguish the real and concrete from the abstract or the possible. Both the observable world and the world of possibility become interesting problems.
2. Through the ability to test *hypotheses*, scientific reasoning emerges. Hypothetical reasoning enables the adolescent to recognize the notion of falsification; that is, hypotheses can be generated and then eliminated as unsupportable, no matter how possible. Indeed, the adolescent spends time attempting to identify the impossible—a fascinating task in itself.
3. The adolescent can now think about the *future* by planning and exploring the possibilities of causation.
4. *Thinking about thoughts* is now possible. The adolescent becomes aware of cognitive activities and mechanisms that make the cognitive process efficient or inefficient and spends time considering the internal cognitive regulation of how and what one thinks. Thus, introspection (or self-examination) becomes an integral part of everyday life.
5. Finally, the sophistication of formal operations opens the door to new

topics—and an *expansion* of thought. Horizons broaden, not the least of which include religion, justice, morality, and identity.

The development of such reasoning is gradual. Some adolescents may reason in this fashion at an early age; for others, it begins later. Some scientists assert that many people never develop abstract reasoning abilities. Most agree, however, that some shift typically occurs during early adolescence. Those adolescents who begin to make this transition do not necessarily use abstract reasoning in all arenas, however. Some may develop abstract reasoning ability in social relations or in making moral judgments, but not, for example, in mathematical reasoning.

CONSEQUENCES OF NEW THINKING CAPACITY

Though we cannot be precise about its exact sequencing, the capacity to engage in the "formal operations" just described helps to explain the advent of many youth behaviors. Four are noted here:

1. With formal operations comes the ability to see oneself through others' eyes. That is, one can take the perspective of other people. This could help explain the tendency for some young adolescents to become introspective or overconcerned about the impression they make on other people.

2. With formal operations comes the concept of the ideal and the chasm that yawns between the real and the ideal. Suddenly the world becomes accountable in a new way. If the ideal can be conceived, the young person reasons, then the ideal must be reachable. With this kind of reasoning, we begin to find young people criticizing social institutions, including the family. Some cultural historians believe that it is this kind of newfound idealism that drives youth to join political movements such as the civil rights movement of the sixties and the peace movement that followed.

3. The insight that the world can be different leads some young people to question the values and norms they used to accept. They begin to question old, familiar rules and values. If the rules and values do not seem to make sense, the young person may discard them or suspend them temporarily. Later, these rules and values are often "reinvented" as the young person rediscovers their truth or appropriateness through experience.

4. As we have already noted, great variability exists in the age at which young adolescents develop formal operations, and passage through this transformation is not necessarily consistent or easy. One noted developmental psychologist, David Elkind, describes the "pseudostupidity" of some young adolescents who move frequently and unpredictably back and forth between forms of childish thought and newly acquired forms of thought.[4]

With this discussion as background, we begin our excursion into the afore-mentioned developmental areas: autonomy, social competence, identity, achievement, and sexuality.

AUTONOMY

Human life begins with total dependence on others for sustenance. One task of growing up is to reduce the dimensions of dependence—to gain the ability to act independently and to make decisions for oneself. To succeed, the process must involve parents' letting go of absolute control while the young person begins to assume more responsibility. The growth toward autonomy does not demand that ties with parents be broken, however. Although responsibility for decisions about day-to-day activities gradually shifts from parents to child, the attachments of affection and care between parents and children can, and frequently do, remain constant as greater behavioral independence is achieved.[5]

GAINING AUTONOMY

The desire of children to move toward greater independence grows rapidly during early adolescence. Our survey asked students to rate the importance of each of twenty-four value statements or goals. One of these was "To make my own decisions." The importance they placed on this value changed more between fifth and ninth grades than any other value statement. Across the five years of early adolescence, the importance of making one's own decisions grows (see Figure 4)[6] more dramatically than any other value area. By the eighth grade, six out of ten young adolescents place high importance on autonomy. No essential difference exists between boys and girls here; at each grade level, they express equal interest in autonomy.

Though the need for autonomy increases dramatically with grade, the attainment of that autonomy does not increase at the same rate. The following statement and adolescent responses bear that out.

	5th	6th	7th	8th	9th
My parents let me make my own decisions.					
Percent who respond "often true" or "very often true"					
Boys	33	36	38	38	42
Girls	30	32	34	40	37

Figure 4 Desire for Autonomy

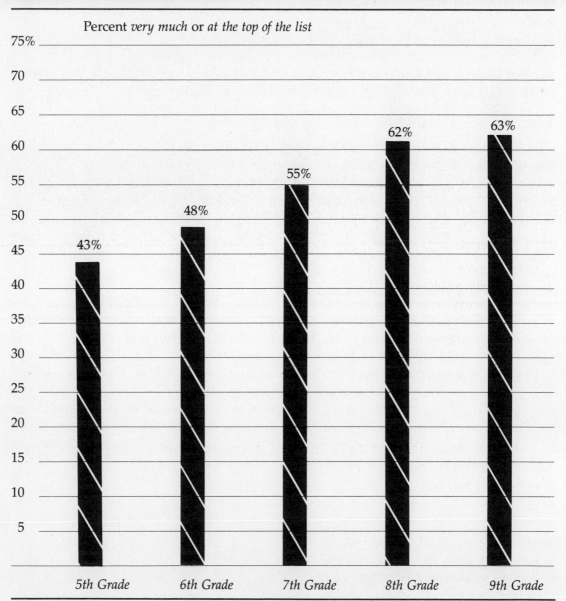

Percent *very much* or *at the top of the list*

Of all the things you want in life, how much do you want to make your own decisions?
At the top of the list
Very much
Quite a bit
Somewhat
Very little or not at all

Overall, only about one third of young adolescents report significant achievement of independence, though nearly two thirds desire it. Notably, girls perceive slightly less attainment of autonomy than do boys, except at the eighth grade level, a discovery that seems to confirm the widely held assumption that parents are more protective of daughters than sons. Information from the parent surveys corroborates the finding that autonomy increases with grade in school. However, neither mother nor father reports that boys achieve greater autonomy than girls.[7] In parents' eyes, boys and girls are allowed equal autonomy.

PARENT-YOUTH CONFLICT

It would seem from the findings reported above that we have the essential ingredients for conflict—young adolescents wanting more autonomy than parents are willing to give. To what extent does this gap between expectations and reality put young adolescents and parents at odds? Much of the literature on adolescents of high school age assumes that parent-child conflict is abundant. However, information from our study does not support this claim for younger adolescents and their parents. What happens, then, in the ten-through-fourteen age period?

Three important findings stand out:[8]

· The amount of youth-parent conflict (the degree to which young adolescents reject or question parental authority) increases slightly between each of the grades from fifth through ninth.
· No major difference exists between boys and girls in the degree of conflict.
· Only a minority of young adolescents report major conflict with parents. Even in ninth grade, less than 20 percent of young adolescents appear to experience strong conflict with parents, and the percentages are even lower for earlier grades. For example, note the percentage of young adolescents who disagree with the following statement:

	5th	*6th*	*7th*	*8th*	*9th*
My parents know what is best for me.					
Percent of boys who disagree	7	8	11	15	17
Percent of girls who disagree	6	8	11	13	19

Mothers and fathers corroborate this pattern of findings. Whether we rely on child or on parent data, we see no evidence that parent-child conflict is widespread.[9] Although conflict is more common by ninth grade, the phenomenon of out-and-out rebellion against parents or rejection of parental values is relatively rare.[10] Autonomy may come more slowly than young adolescents would prefer, but the pace does not seem to call into serious question either the authority of parents or the affectional bonds between young adolescents and their parents. In sum, little evidence appears here to support the claim that a significant "generation gap" begins during this age period.

Though families of young adolescents are not marked by serious antagonism between parents and children, some of these feelings, including anger and hostility, are to be expected. Anger does not negate love; indeed, they often coexist. We would expect most feelings of anger to occur in those grades where the gap is widest between the level of desired autonomy and the level of attained autonomy, that is, in the eighth and ninth grade. Figure 5 confirms this prediction. Note, however, that the grade-by-grade increase in anger is more pronounced for girls than for boys. This difference may reflect a social climate that encourages girls more than boys to acknowledge or express negative feelings, or it may stem from the fact that girls are subjected to more rules governing their behavior than are boys.

SOCIAL COMPETENCE

The development of social competence is a crucial part of maturation. To be able to create and maintain lasting, meaningful relationships with others requires a number of social skills. In this section, we look at young adolescent development in terms of three important competencies: the ability to self-disclose, to empathize, and to make friends.

SELF-DISCLOSURE

The following two survey items addressed the issue of young adolescents' ability to talk to others about personal matters.

	5th	6th	7th	8th	9th
I can't talk about personal things with my friends.					
Percent who answer "quite true" or "very true"					
Boys	31	26	23	22	20
Girls	24	20	16	13	12
It's hard for me to share my feelings with other people.					
Percent who answer "often true" or "very often true"					
Boys	34	27	22	19	15
Girls	25	20	14	12	9

Figure 5   Anger Toward Parents

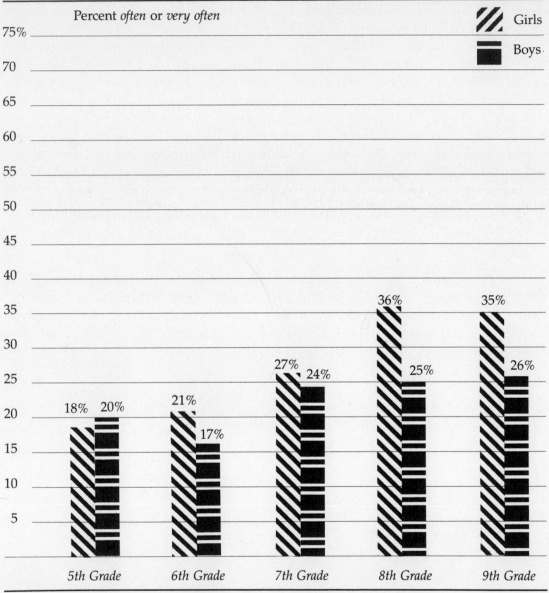

Percent *often* or *very often*

Girls
Boys

Grade	Girls	Boys
5th Grade	18%	20%
6th Grade	21%	17%
7th Grade	27%	24%
8th Grade	36%	25%
9th Grade	35%	26%

I get mad at my parent(s) or guardian(s)

Very often   Once in a while
Often   Never
Sometimes

Boys and girls make approximately equal progress across the five years in developing the ability to self-disclose. Fifth-grade girls report slightly more of this ability than fifth-grade boys, and this difference remains fairly stable across the five years of early adolescence. Overall, the vast majority of young adolescents report they *do* have the ability to share feelings with others.

EMPATHY

Empathy is a complex capacity, and difficult to measure in a survey, but two survey items reflected aspects of it.

	5th	*6th*	*7th*	*8th*	*9th*
It is hard for me to understand what other people are feeling.					
Percent who answer "quite true" or "very often true"					
Boys	34	27	22	19	15
Girls	25	20	14	12	9
I know what my best friend is feeling before he or she tells me.					
Percent who answer "often true" or "very often true"					
Boys	26	29	27	31	32
Girls	26	28	37	41	49

On both items, girls report more ability to understand the feelings of others than do boys, although both boys and girls make progress on empathy-related skills between fifth and ninth grade. On sensing the feelings of a friend, girls make great strides between the seventh and ninth grades, while boys make little progress. By the ninth grade, about one half of the girls and about one third of boys can intuitively connect with the feelings of a best friend.

MAKING FRIENDS

In a third social competency—ease of making friends—girls again report slightly more ability than boys, as shown by adolescent responses to this statement.

	5th	*6th*	*7th*	*8th*	*9th*
I have a hard time making friends.					
Percent who answer "often true" or "very often true"					
Boys	25	21	20	18	22
Girls	21	16	15	14	13

The patterns that occur across these three social competencies—self-disclosure, empathy, and making friends—are similar and worth noting.

· Both boys and girls report increased competence on all three between the fifth and ninth grades.
· In all cases, girls report more competence than boys.
· The difference between boys and girls in social competence usually is visible by the fifth grade, and this difference tends to be maintained through the years of early adolescence.

SOCIAL ALIENATION

Overall, the majority of young adolescents in this study report having competencies crucial for developing lasting bonds with other people. In addition, the vast majority have close friends; 85 percent of them report having three or more close friends. Only 15 percent report having two or fewer friends.

About 15 percent of young adolescents also experience social alienation or estrangement from others, as shown below. Note that boys are slightly more likely than girls to agree with each of the three statements, and fifth graders are more likely to agree than older youth.[11]

	5th	6th	7th	8th	9th
I am a lonely person.					
Percent who answer "often" or "almost always" true					
Boys	14	11	12	10	11
Girls	11	8	9	7	11
I feel no one understands me.					
Percent who answer "often" or "almost always" true					
Boys	23	18	17	17	19
Girls	21	17	16	15	17
At school, kids make fun of me.					
Percent who answer "often" or "very often" true					
Boys	21	16	15	15	14
Girls	13	12	8	7	7

Young adolescents who experience social alienation are at risk. We find that highly alienated youth tend to have low self-esteem, experience a high degree of peer pressure toward negative behaviors, and are prone to antisocial behavior and thoughts of suicide.[12] Though the percentage who feel alienated is relatively low, these young adolescents need particular care and concern. Meaningful social networks, both formal and informal, are especially important, for through these networks young adolescents begin to acquire all-important life-affirming values.[13]

Unfortunately, the family itself may be one source of social alienation. We find that low parental nurturance, high authoritarian control, high coercive punishment, and low family closeness are all related to the social alienation of a young person. (For further description of family dynamics, see Chapter 15). Families that demonstrate these patterns apparently fail to equip a child with the confidence and skills necessary for connecting with others outside the family unit.[14]

BOY-GIRL DIFFERENCES IN SOCIAL COMPETENCE

Across our various measures of social competence, girls consistently show more skill than boys. Observers of human development see, increasingly, that men and women differ in their life experiences and life perspectives, and it can be argued that social competence is one part of a larger constellation of skills and values on which males and females tend to differ. The lives of women are more marked by a desire for, and attainment of, meaningful connections with other people. The lives of men tend to be characterized more by individualism and a greater separateness from people. These are not necessarily differences that are true of every individual man or woman but, rather, are tendencies that consistently appear when large groups of men and women are compared.[15] Other research on adolescents and adults document these differences. What we are seeing in this study is some evidence that these differences are also visible during early adolescence. The difference in social competence is but one example. Another is the difference between the sexes in the influence of friends. Other such differences will be seen in those chapters that discuss worries, values, social attitudes, and prosocial behavior.

IDENTITY

A third developmental task that touches the life of the young adolescent is the formation of identity. We have chosen to treat this complex phenomenon as the process of self-definition. We can expect identity to be an issue during early adolescence for several reasons. First, changes brought on by biological matura-tion demand a reassessment of who one is and how these changes relate to other aspects of the self. Second, the acquisition of new thinking processes allows young adolescents to reflect on how they are seen by others. Young people then incorporate this new information into their definition of self. Third, as we have seen, young adolescents achieve changes in autonomy. With these changes comes experience in new arenas, and their performance in these new areas gives young adolescents additional information about themselves.

In this section, we look at four aspects of the self: the development of self-concept, body image, self-esteem, and sex-role orientation.

IMPORTANCE OF POSITIVE VIEW OF SELF

Young adolescents place high value on attaining a positive self-concept, as the responses to the following question show.

	5th	6th	7th	8th	9th
How important is it to you "to feel good about myself"?					
Percent who respond "very much" or "at the top of my list"					
Boys	71	71	74	74	75
Girls	74	77	78	81	82

This value is high for all grades, with a slight increase in value between the fifth and ninth grades for both boys and girls. However, girls assign it a slightly higher value than boys.[16] Though positive self-regard is of high importance to them, most young adolescents apparently do not spend a great deal of time reflecting on their identity, as suggested by the following:

	5th	6th	7th	8th	9th	Total
I spend a lot of time thinking about who I am.						
Percent who respond "quite true" or "very true"						
Boys	26	26	27	27	38	28
Girls	32	31	30	34	42	33

About a third of young adolescents report frequent reflection on the self, with a major increase between eighth and ninth grades, and with girls again dwelling on this factor slightly more than boys.[17] Interest in self-concept is likely to increase through the high school years as the cognitive processes necessary for abstract reasoning continue to develop.

BODY IMAGE

One of the major events of early adolescence is biological maturation, a process that causes changes in weight, height, and body form. Responses to the following statement refer to satisfaction with one's body.

	5th	6th	7th	8th	9th	Total
I feel good about my body. Percent who respond "often true" or "very often true"						
Boys	62	61	58	58	58	59
Girls	52	47	43	41	41	45

At all grade levels, girls express less satisfaction with their bodies than do boys, and girls' satisfaction level decreases across the five years, while boys' stays relatively stable.[18]

At least two processes may explain these findings. First, our culture encourages girls more than boys to be concerned about body appearance. Females, even by the age of ten, are evaluated by others more on the basis of physical characteristics than are boys. These cultural expectations for girls create a larger discrepancy for girls than boys between their ideal body image and the image they see in the mirror. Secondly, girls proceed through the process of biological maturation about two years ahead of boys, so at any point in the early adolescent years, more girls than boys will be experiencing the kinds of physical changes that cause self-consciousness about one's body.

SELF-ESTEEM

At this period of life a young adolescent must adapt to a bewildering variety of biological and social change. Therefore, it seems reasonable to expect major changes in overall self-esteem—the degree to which one feels like a person of worth. The index of self-esteem which follows is an average of six items (1 = low, 5 = high).

	5th	6th	7th	8th	9th
Boys	3.88	3.96	3.93	3.94	3.92
Girls	3.81	3.86	3.82	3.81	3.81

Contrary to expectation, we find no grade-related change in self-esteem. Self-esteem remains stable across the five years for both boys and girls as this index shows. It may be, as others have suggested, that self-esteem increases after the transition from early adolescence to later adolescence.[19] These figures show a slight but persistent trend for boys to claim higher self-esteem than girls.[20] Again, more than one explanation for this difference is possible. The differences in body satisfaction described earlier may generalize to one's total sense of self-worth. Or, as one observer of girl-boy differences suggests, young adolescent girls may now begin to see the female experience and the sense of connection that is at the heart of female consciousness undervalued in adult society so that at this age girls begin a process of self-effacement.[21]

SEX-ROLE ORIENTATION

The degree to which one adopts or exhibits masculine and feminine traits determines one's sex-role orientation. Traits viewed as masculine and feminine are defined by social convention or social norms. In present-day U.S. society, individuality, assertiveness, competitiveness, and independence are expected of boys, while nurturance, emotional expressiveness, and interpersonal competence are expected of girls. Socialization to these orientations begins during infancy and continues throughout the childhood years.

Development of preference for sex-role orientations during early adolescence is not well understood. To enable us to look at these questions, we included scales for both feminine and masculine sex roles in this study. We discovered that, between fifth and ninth grade, boys experience a *modest increase* in a masculine sex-role orientation and a modest decrease in a feminine orientation.[22] Among girls between the fifth and ninth grades, masculine and feminine sex-role orientations remain relatively stable.

	Androgynous	*Feminine*	*Masculine*	*Undifferentiated*
Boys in each category by grade				
5th	24%	16%	26%	34%
6th	30%	14%	27%	29%
7th	28%	11%	31%	29%
8th	30%	9%	35%	26%
9th	33%	11%	31%	25%
Total boys	29%	12%	30%	29%

	Androgynous	*Feminine*	*Masculine*	*Undifferentiated*
Girls in each category by grade				
5th	30%	32%	13%	25%
6th	35%	31%	12%	23%
7th	39%	28%	12%	21%
8th	43%	29%	10%	19%
9th	47%	31%	9%	14%
Total girls	39%	30%	11%	20%

We determined the percentage of young adolescents who appear in four sex-type categories representing combinations of masculine and feminine traits: androgynous (high on both masculine and feminine orientation), masculine (high on masculine, low on feminine), feminine (high on feminine, low on masculine), and undifferentiated (low on both).[23] Both boys and girls become more androgynous between the fifth and ninth grades, with the increase being sharper for girls. Overall, 29 percent of boys and 39 percent of girls are androgynous. The androgynous person has certain advantages, including the flexibility to act competently in both achievement-oriented settings and nurturance-oriented settings. In modern society, androgyny may well be an important component of social and emotional well-being.[24]

ACHIEVEMENT

In the context of development, achievement has two meanings: (a) to develop the motivation to work up to one's capacity and (b) to develop meaningful goals or aspirations for the future. These are particularly important values in Western culture. Parents and other socializing agents seek to instill these values in new generations. According to young adolescents in this study, parents tend to increase the pressure for achievement between the fifth and ninth grades. We created a scale measuring the average amount of parental pressure for achievement that young adolescents experience (1 = low; 5 = high). The pattern is shown here:

	5th	*6th*	*7th*	*8th*	*9th*
Boys	3.59	3.81	3.82	3.82	3.78
Girls	3.33	3.48	3.64	3.62	3.72

We can see that pressure for achievement, as perceived by young adolescents, increases with grade, peaking for boys in the seventh and eighth grades and peaking for girls in the ninth grade. In addition, more pressure for achievement is perceived by boys than by girls. Note, however, that the difference in perception between boys and girls nearly disappears by ninth grade.[25] (For further discussion of parental pressure, see Chapter 15.)

From this perceptual pattern, we might expect achievement levels to increase with grade as well, and to be higher for boys than for girls. The actual findings for the two correlates of achievement—achievement motivation and future aspirations—follow.

ACHIEVEMENT MOTIVATION

We created an index of motivation to achieve by averaging four items dealing with how much one attempts to work up to one's abilities, particularly in the school context. Components of achievement motivation are: agreement that "It bothers me when I don't do something well," that "When things get tough, I keep trying," that "At school I try as hard as I can to do my best work," and placing high value on "To do well in school." The index of motivation to achieve was as follows (1 = low; 5 = high):

	5th	6th	7th	8th	9th
Average for boys	3.88	3.86	3.80	3.81	3.74
Average for girls	3.97	4.00	3.97	3.96	3.92

Contrary to the expectations suggested above, we find that, for boys, achievement motivation slightly declines with grade and that girls have higher achievement motivation than boys at each grade level.[26]

FUTURE ASPIRATIONS

Educational aspirations tend to increase during early adolescence, but are more pronounced for girls than for boys.[27] Figure 6 shows this pattern. As with achievement motivation, girls, more often than boys, report high educational aspirations at each grade. And, consistent with this finding, girls are more likely than boys, at each grade, to "think about what I will do when I am an adult."

Clearly, across several measures, girls report higher achievement motivation and aspiration than do boys. What accounts for this contradiction in the connection between perceiving pressure to achieve and having achievement motivation? One possibility may be that parents put greater pressure on boys than on girls because boys exhibit less achievement. This is consistent with the finding, reported in Chapter 2, that boys show less interest in school than girls. Accordingly, parents may more strongly urge boys to achieve.

Another possibility is that some parents may pressure their sons because they hold the traditional assumption that boys must be prepared to provide for a family, while girls need only marry the right provider.

SEXUALITY

Puberty is distinguished by a relatively rapid rate of major biological and physical change beginning in early adolescence. In general terms, four types of change occur during puberty: a spurt in physical growth, maturation of reproductive organs, changes in the endocrine system, and the development of secondary sex characteristics such as pubic hair, breast development for girls, and voice changes and facial hair for boys.[28] In the overall sequence of pubertal changes, girls tend to develop about two years earlier than boys.

The mothers in this study were asked to place their child along a continuum of progress through puberty. Here are the percentages of boys and girls at each stage as reported by their mothers.

	Boys					*Girls*				
	5th	*6th*	*7th*	*8th*	*9th*	*5th*	*6th*	*7th*	*8th*	*9th*
Percent not yet begun	86	65	38	15	5	33	14	5	1	1
Percent beginning	14	31	48	44	18	58	56	42	18	6
Percent in the middle	0	3	11	26	41	7	22	31	31	21
Percent almost through	0	1	3	13	29	2	5	13	29	35
Percent completely through	0	0	0	3	7	1	3	9	20	37

Girls at each grade level are further along in the pubertal cycle than boys, with the difference lessening in the eighth and ninth grades. These pubertal changes require considerable adaptation by young adolescents. The changes affect a number of areas, including body image, self-concept, interpersonal relationships, relationships to parents, and moods. No doubt pubertal development also triggers psychological conflicts around the issues of sexual motives and sexual behavior.

This section explores five topics in the area of young adolescent sexuality:

Figure 6 Educational Aspirations

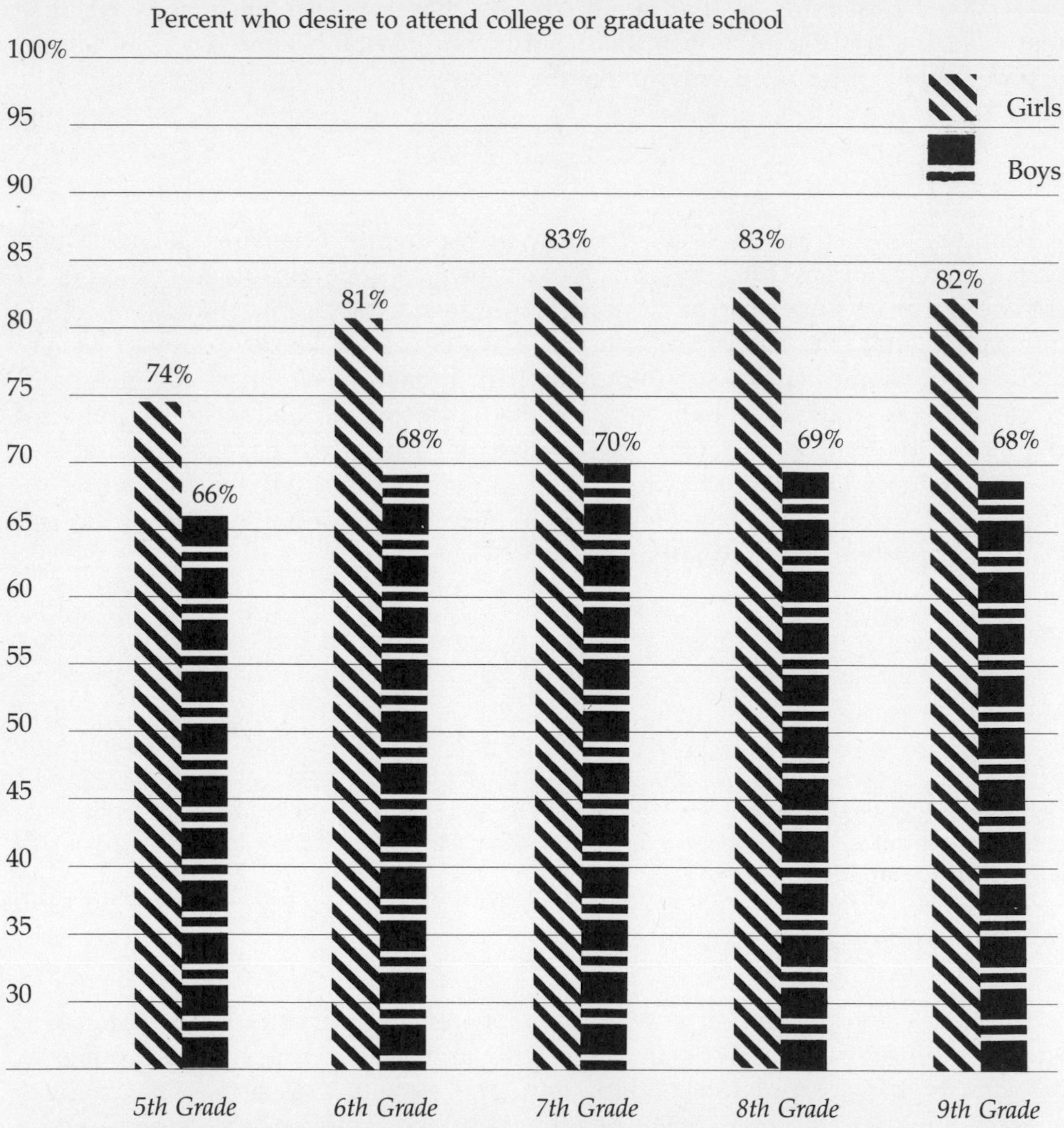

Percent who desire to attend college or graduate school

How many more years do you think you will go to school? Choose the statement that fits you best.

I would like to quit school as soon as I can.

I plan to finish high school but don't think I'll go to college.

I'd like to go to some kind of trade school or vocational school after high school.

I'd like to go to college after high school.

I'd like to go to college and then go on after college and study to be something like a lawyer, doctor, professor, scientist, minister or priest.

frequency of thinking and talking about sex, interest in the opposite sex, intimacy, attitudes toward and experience of sexual intercourse, and communication with parents about sex.

THINKING AND TALKING ABOUT SEX

The frequency of thinking and talking about sex increases with each grade for both boys and girls, as shown in Figure 7. The percentages for thinking about sex are lower than for talking about it, suggesting that "thinking about sex" was understood to be a solitary activity. Not only do the percentages increase with every grade for both thinking and talking, but at every grade level the percentages are also higher for boys than for girls.

The increases in thinking and talking about sex certainly have something to do with the onset of puberty. Note, however, that as early as fifth grade, approximately one quarter of young adolescents report frequent talking and thinking about sex. Curiosity about the topic of sex clearly predates puberty, particularly for boys.

INTEREST IN THE OPPOSITE SEX

Figure 8 shows the percentage of young adolescents who responded positively to the question, "How much do you like to go to parties or dances where there are both boys and girls?" Interest rises steadily between fifth and ninth grade. Moreover, a sizable proportion of fifth graders have this interest. Many adults will remember that fifth grade was a time when they purposely kept a distance between themselves and the opposite sex. It may be that we are seeing evidence of a major cultural change in this phenomenon. (On the other hand, the "purposeful distance" we kept may have signaled the dawning of real interest for ourselves at the time.)

Recall here the finding reported in Chapter 2 about the sex composition of friendship circles.

	5th	6th	7th	8th	9th
Of your best friends (kids your own age), how many are members of the opposite sex?					
Percent who respond "half or more"					
Boys	30	36	44	53	62
Girls	32	36	42	49	53

The increase in opposite-sex friendships provides a second indication that

Figure 7   Frequency of Thinking and Talking About Sex

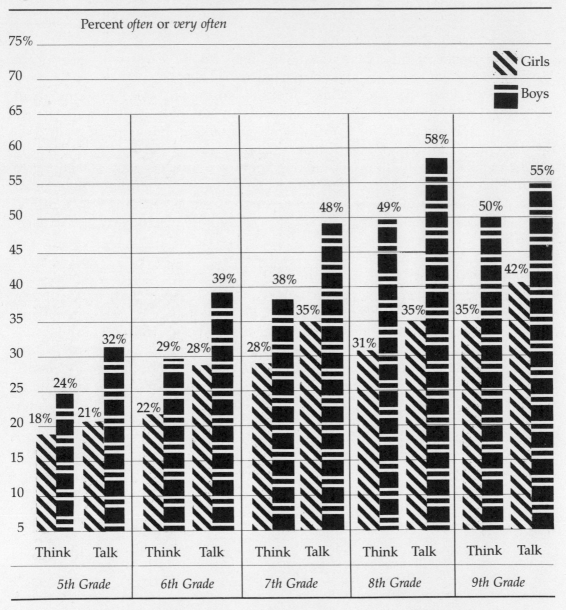

Percent *often* or *very often*

How often do you think about sex?
How often do your friends talk about sex?

Never
Once in a while
Sometimes

Very often
Often

Figure 8   Interest in Attending Sex-Integrated Parties

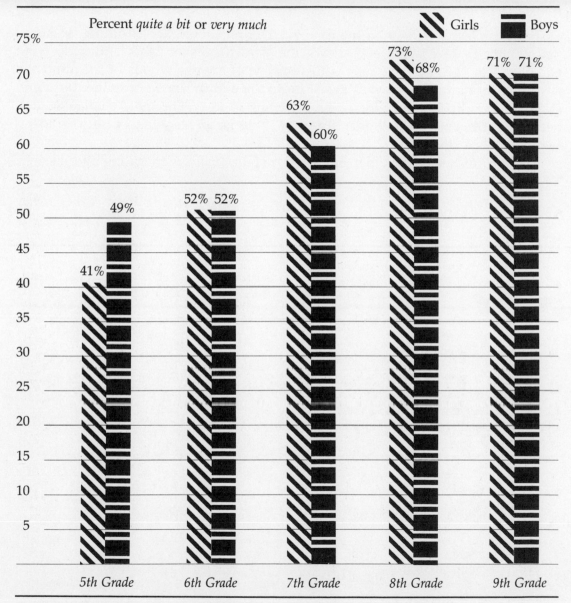

How much do you like to go to parties or dances where there are both boys and girls?

Very much	A little	Not at all
Quite a bit		
Some		

interest in the opposite sex increases with grade level and that fifth-grade boys and girls do not all seek to avoid each other.

INTIMACY

Early adolescence is often the time for the first experience of dating, kissing, and falling in love. Figure 9 shows the percentages of boys and girls who affirmed that "I am in love now with someone of my age who is of the opposite sex." There is an increase with grade up to the eighth. In every grade, boys are slightly more likely than girls to report being in love. The most change occurs between fifth and sixth grade. Even so, a large percentage of fifth graders respond affirmatively.

The figures below show percentages for involvement with dating and kissing.

	5th	6th	7th	8th	9th
In the last twelve months, how many times have you been out on a date (such as going out to a party or movie with one person of the opposite sex)?					
Boys					
Percent 1–5 times	21	24	29	37	33
Percent 6 or more times	12	11	16	23	34
Girls					
Percent 1–5 times	13	17	24	28	29
Percent 6 or more times	6	5	8	15	25
In the last twelve months, how many times have you kissed someone about your age who is of the opposite sex?					
Boys					
Percent 1–5 times	22	24	27	30	27
Percent 6–19 times	8	10	12	18	18
Percent 20 or more times	6	7	11	15	26
Girls					
Percent 1–5 times	16	22	25	28	30
Percent 6–19 times	4	6	8	12	17
Percent 20 or more times	3	2	6	11	26

Based on these figures, and Figure 9, several patterns stand out:[29]

· The percentage of young adolescents who report being in love increases predictably with grade (up to the eighth).

Figure 9   Young Adolescents in Love

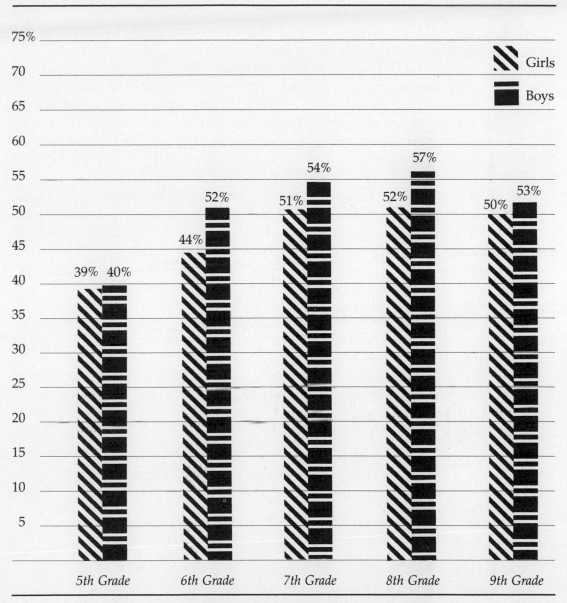

I am in love now with someone my age who is of the opposite sex.

Yes
No

· In every grade, boys are slightly more likely than girls to report being in love.
· A higher percentage of boys than girls report experience with dating and kissing.
· A relatively constant grade-by-grade rise occurs in dating and kissing, as seen in the percentages for the one-to-five-times ranges.
· When we look at higher frequencies (six dates or more, kissing twenty or more times), we see a major increase between the eighth and ninth grades.
· More fifth graders report being in love, dating, and kissing than adults might expect. Nearly 40 percent report being in love, and more than one in four fifth graders report dating and/or kissing in the last twelve months.

SEXUAL INTERCOURSE

Figure 10 shows the percentages of young adolescents who agree or strongly agree with the statement, "I don't think that I will have sexual intercourse (make love, "go all the way") with someone until I get married." Between the sixth and ninth grades, there is a grade by grade decrease in agreement with the statement, but the decrease is more pronounced among boys than among girls. In fact, differences on this issue point up one of the largest attitudinal differences between boys and girls in the entire survey. (The fifth-grade figures may reflect, in part, an incomplete understanding of the term *sexual intercourse*, and the jump in agreement with the statement between fifth and sixth grade may reflect greater clarity.)

The youth survey also asked a carefully worded question about the experience of sexual intercourse. Responses for boys and girls combined are as follows:

	5th	6th	7th	8th	9th
Have you ever had sexual intercourse ("gone all the way" or "made love")?					
Percent who respond					
Never	73	79	82	81	78
I don't know what sexual intercourse is	10	4	3	2	2
Yes, one time	8	6	6	6	6
Yes, 2–5 times	5	6	5	6	7
Yes, 6 times or more	4	4	4	5	7

When we combine the three yes categories given above, these are the percentages of young adolescents who report engaging in intercourse one or more times:

Figure 10   Percentage Opposed to Premarital Intercourse

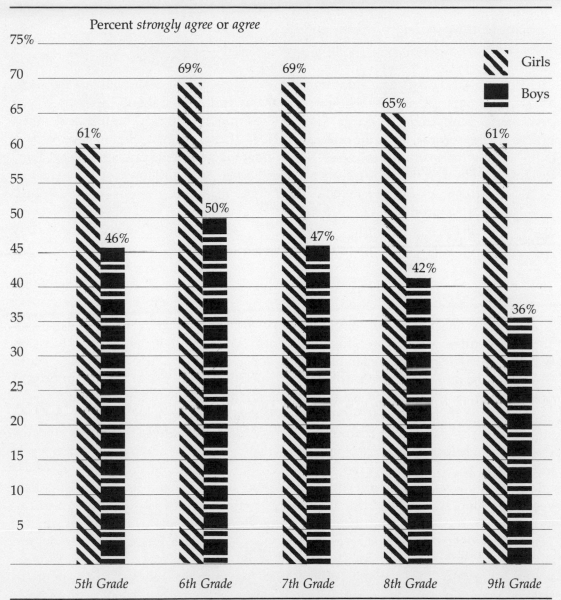

Percent *strongly agree* or *agree*

Girls

Boys

5th Grade: 61%, 46%
6th Grade: 69%, 50%
7th Grade: 69%, 47%
8th Grade: 65%, 42%
9th Grade: 61%, 36%

I don't think I will have sexual intercourse (make love, "go all the way") with someone until I get married.
Strongly agree   Not sure   Disagree
Agree   Strongly disagree

	5th	6th	7th	8th	9th
Percent reporting sexual intercourse one or more times	17	16	15	17	20

The fifth- and sixth-grade data may reflect, again, uncertainty about the term *sexual intercourse*. Conceivably, some of these youth mistakenly answered yes because they misunderstood the term.[30] Presumably, though, eighth and ninth graders know what is being asked, and of these, nearly one in five report experience with sexual intercourse. The percentages of boys and girls who claim to have engaged in intercourse one or more times are as follows:

	7th	8th	9th
Percent reporting sexual intercourse one or more times			
Boys	22	26	28
Girls	9	9	13

The differences between boys and girls are quite large, and other research shows a similar pattern, in which experience with intercourse was found to be two or three times greater for boys than for girls.[31] Why this difference occurs is unclear. In part it may reflect American society's greater tolerance of, and even greater encouragement of, sexual experimentation by boys than by girls.

Are the data on sexual intercourse believable? American culture tends to stigmatize sexually active girls more than it does sexually active boys: lack of virginity suggests a character flaw in girls, while lack of virginity in boys is more likely to be seen as a temporary lack of judgment, or as part of a "boys-will-be-boys" syndrome, or even as a normal part of sexual development. Presumably, then, there are boys for whom sexual activity is something to brag about—a sign of manhood that they think elevates them in the eyes of others. This double standard, which research shows still exists but to a lesser degree than in previous generations, could lead some young adolescent males to *over-report* experience with sexual intercourse. Accordingly, the sexual intercourse data of boys may be somewhat distorted. But a tendency on the part of some to overreport experience with sexual intercourse may be offset by others who underreport sexual activity for fear that a parent or other adult might find out how they responded. In any case, we must recognize that these sexual intercourse data are consistent with data reported in other research projects.[32]

RELATIONSHIP OF SEXUAL INTERCOURSE TO OTHER FACTORS

Responses to the sexual intercourse item are correlated very strongly with other variables, including scales on chemical use and antisocial behavior.[33] The sexually active in this study tend also to be involved in a number of deviations from adult norms and expectations about appropriate behavior for young adolescents. All three factors (sexual intercourse, chemical use, and antisocial behavior) are tied to similar family and value patterns—young adolescents who are deeply involved in any of these three behaviors tend to place less emphasis on church and religion, to have lower achievement motivation, and to receive less nurturance and support from parents.

COMMUNICATION WITH PARENTS

The data in this section on sexuality show quite strongly that interest in, and expression of, various forms of sexuality is an important part of young adolescents' lives, even among fifth graders. Unfortunately, the numbers in Figure 11 suggest that most parents do not discuss sexuality with their children in any meaningful way, and as a result, young persons' development, thought, conversation, and experimentation in the area of sexuality takes place without benefit of parental wisdom and guidance.

While a modest increase in "good talks" with parents does take place across the five grades, the data of Figure 11 affirm the common assumption that girls receive more parental guidance than boys do. This holds for each of the five grades. However, if inclination to sexual interest and activity is a yardstick by which to measure the need for discussion with parents, then it is boys who need it most.

SUMMARY

A number of significant developmental processes are occurring at the same time as young people pass from the fifth to the ninth grade. These changes are summarized below.

These decrease for both boys and girls:
      Satisfaction with body
      Motivation to achieve
      Opposition to premarital sexual intercourse
These increase for both boys and girls:
      Need for autonomy
      Attainment of autonomy
      Youth-parent conflict

Figure 11   Good Talks with Parents About Sex

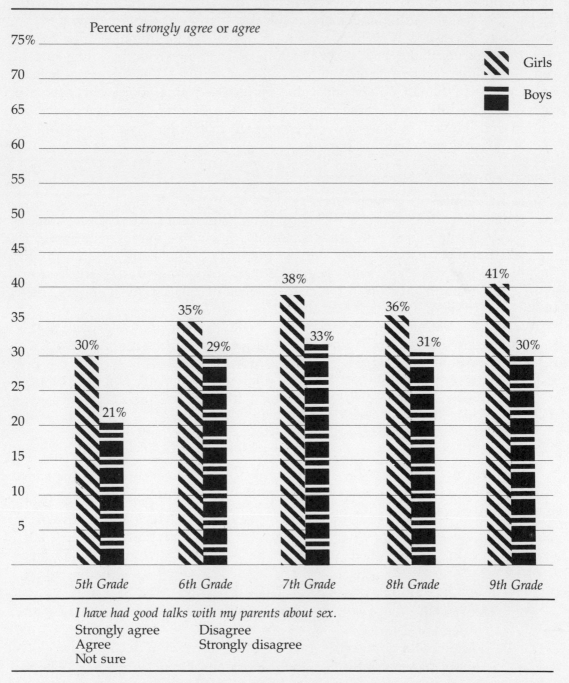

Percent *strongly agree* or *agree*

Girls

Boys

75%
70
65
60
55
50
45
40
35
30
25
20
15
10
5

	5th Grade	6th Grade	7th Grade	8th Grade	9th Grade
Girls	30%	35%	38%	36%	41%
Boys	21%	29%	33%	31%	30%

I have had good talks with my parents about sex.
Strongly agree   Disagree
Agree   Strongly disagree
Not sure

Ability to self-disclose
Understanding of other people's feelings
Ease of making friends
Importance of positive self-image
Masculine sex-role orientation
Parental pressure to achieve
Educational aspirations
Frequency of thinking about sex
Interest in the opposite sex
Being "in love"
Dating
Incidence of kissing

It is more typical of boys to
Experience social alienation (loneliness, etc.)
Have slightly higher self-esteem
Experience more pressure to achieve
Think frequently about sex
Be "in love"
Kiss
Be involved in sexual intercourse

It is more typical of girls to
Feel anger at parents
Experience greater decrease in body satisfaction
Increase in feminine sex-role orientation
Have higher motivation to achieve
Have higher educational aspirations
Contemplate the future
Be opposed to premarital sexual intercourse
Have conversations with parents about sex

When looking at all the changes that occur during this period—those listed above as well as changes in body size and shape and in ways of thinking—one cannot help being struck with the sheer number of adaptations the young adolescent faces. No wonder there is turmoil. No wonder young adolescents sometimes seem overwhelmed and behave in ways that seem irrational to adults. They have a right to feel overwhelmed. There is a lot going on.

Another difficulty young adolescents face is the great variety among the peers who play such an important role in shaping their thinking and acting. At the very time when being like others takes on enormous significance, they look around them and find any number of ways in which they are unlike their friends.

The "typical" eighth grader simply does not exist. The timing of a host of changes—biological, cognitive, emotional, social—varies widely, and even the sequencing of these changes differs from individual to individual. This variety, combined with their new ways of thinking about themselves and relating to others, is the source of the inconsistency, emotionalism, increased energy, and questioning of adult values and perspectives that leads some people to refer to any gathering of young adolescents, and particularly seventh and eighth graders, as a zoo. Teachers and youth group leaders who have not had previous experience in working with this age group frequently find that, although person-to-person contact with young adolescents is wonderfully satisfying, working with them in group settings can be chaotic, frustrating, and both physically and emotionally draining.

CHAPTER 4

Worries and Concerns

· From a list of twenty potential sources of worry, young adolescents worry most often about how they're doing in school, their looks, and how their friends treat them.
· Nearly one out of every four fifth graders worries about the possibility of sexual abuse.
· Worry about peer relationships increases with age.
· Parents radically *under*estimate the extent to which young adolescents worry about destructive or harmful events and forces.
· Parents *over*estimate the extent to which young adolescents worry about peer relationships.
· On sixteen of the items, fifth graders report more frequent worry than young adolescents in any other grade.

Adults see the evidences of internal conflict, anxiety, tension, and uncertainty in the sometimes explosive and puzzling behavior of young adolescents, but not much is known about the nature of the worries and concerns that give rise to these behaviors. Do young people worry about great global issues like war and poverty, or are their concerns more local and personal? How much do they worry about their relationships with friends and peers? To what extent are they concerned about victimization (for example, sexual abuse, physical abuse at home, physical violence at school)? In this chapter we look at three major issues: the relationship of worries to grade in school, how boys and girls compare in worries, and how much mothers and fathers know about what young adolescents worry about.

WORRIES AND GRADE IN SCHOOL

The survey presented a list of twenty issues and asked students to say how much they worry about each on a five-point scale ranging from "very much" to "not at all." The percentages of youth in each of the five grades responding "very much" or "quite a bit" for each of these issues are listed in Table 4.1.[1]

Table 4.1 Twenty Worries of Young Adolescents

Percent responding that they worried very much *or* quite a bit *about the survey item*

Survey Question	All Youth	Grade 5th	6th	7th	8th	9th
My school performance	56	54	54	56	58	60
My looks	53	42	48	56	60	57
How well other kids like me	48	45	46	51	50	47
That one of my parents might die	47	50	48	49	46	41
How my friends treat me	45	42	43	46	47	45
Hunger and poverty in the U.S.	38	52	41	38	32	31
Violence in the U.S.	36	43	37	38	33	30
That I might lose my best friend	36	40	35	39	34	29
Drugs and drinking around me	35	40	38	35	33	32
That I might not get a good job	30	31	28	31	28	30
Whether my body is growing normally	26	31	28	27	24	17
Nuclear bombing of the U.S.	25	29	28	27	22	21
That my parents might divorce	22	30	26	22	17	13
That I may die soon	21	26	24	24	17	13
Sexual abuse	19	23	21	19	17	14
That friends will get me in trouble	18	25	21	18	13	13
Drinking by a parent	15	21	18	14	11	11
Getting beat up at school	12	18	16	12	9	9
Physical abuse by a parent	12	17	13	12	9	9
That I might kill myself	11	16	12	11	9	9

School performance is the most frequent worry for all youth combined and for young adolescents in all individual grades except the eighth. Worry "about my looks" is the second highest concern of seventh and ninth graders. Of all twenty worry items, this one changes more between fifth and ninth grade than any other worry.[2]

Worry about relationships with friends is high in all five grades. Besides school performance and worry about "my looks," it is the only worry that increases with an increase in age. We see this increase in the items "how well other kids like me" and "how well my friends treat me," and it is consistent with the Chapter 2 finding that the degree of peer influence is also shown to increase with age. Worry about "my looks" may be another expression of concern for peer acceptance. Note that these three worries peak in the eighth grade, with a slight downturn in ninth grade.

Victimization is one of three kinds of worries that are higher for fifth and sixth graders than for seventh, eighth, and ninth graders. Fifth and sixth graders worry more than these older adolescents about physical abuse by a parent, that they might get beat up at school, that friends will get them into trouble, and that they might be sexually abused.

Worry about *national issues of peace and justice* is a second concern that is higher among younger youth. In particular these three issues worry them: hunger and poverty in America, violence in America, and nuclear destruction.

Worry abut *parents* is a third area that is higher among younger youth who worry that their parents might die, that their parents might divorce, or about a parent's drinking.

Overall, younger youth tend to express more worries than older youth. In fact, on sixteen of the twenty questions, fifth graders report the most worry of all the grades. Most of these fifth-grade concerns reflect worry about negative events happening to self, parents, or the nation.

This is a major finding, and it contradicts the oft-expressed opinion (or hope) that exposure to the threats and stresses of the "real world" begins in the junior high years. Instead, children in the fifth grade appear to be very much aware of and highly concerned about global problems. The impact of television and movies, which expose impressionable fifth graders to problems that are made to appear omnipresent, may be reflected here. This exposure to major problems may well create substantial psychological pain for fifth graders, who are at a particularly powerless and vulnerable age.

Twenty-five percent of all youth are worried "very much" or "quite a bit" about the possibility of nuclear destruction. When we add the youth who say they are "somewhat" worried, the figure increases to 47 percent. This burden of concern is a sign of our times, and it is unlikely to diminish with the passage of time. Mounting evidence indicates that fear of nuclear destruction has drastic psychological implications for young people, including lower motivation and an increasing sense of pessimism about the future.[3]

The sexual abuse of children by adults has recently come to public attention as a major national problem, and sexual abuse rates have increased nationally.[4] Nearly one out of every five (19 percent) of these young adolescents worries that "someone might force me to do sexual things I don't want to do." Among fifth graders, 24 percent express this worry.

WORRIES: DIFFERENCES BETWEEN BOYS AND GIRLS

Significant differences appear between boys and girls on eighteen of the twenty worry items. Table 4.2 lists these differences in descending order.

Table 4.2 Sex Differences in Worries of Young Adolescents

	Percent very much *or* quite a bit		
	Percent all boys	Percent all girls	Percent difference between boys and girls
Worries girls report more than boys			
My looks	43	62	19
How well other kids like me	43	53	10
Sexual abuse	14	23	9
That I might lose my best friend	31	40	9
My school performance	54	59	5
How my friends treat me	42	47	5
Hunger and poverty in the U.S.	36	40	4
Drugs and drinking around me	34	37	3
That one of my parents might die	45	48	3
Worries boys report more than girls			
That I might not get a good job	32	27	5
Getting beat up at school	15	10	5
Nuclear bombing of the U.S.	28	23	5
That friends will get me in trouble	20	15	5
Drinking by a parent	17	13	4
Physical abuse by a parent	13	10	3
That I might kill myself	13	10	3

	Percent all boys	Percent all girls	Percent difference between boys and girls
No difference between boys and girls			
Violence in the U.S.	36	36	–
Whether my body is growing normally	26	25	1
That I may die soon	21	21	–
That my parents might divorce	23	21	2

The largest differences between boys and girls occur in three areas: worry about looks, worry about how well other kids like them, and worry about sexual abuse.

In all three cases, girls report more worry than boys, and this difference remains fairly constant across the five grades. Other areas in which girls express more worry than boys include school performance and peer relationships ("That I might lose my best friend," and "How my friends treat me"). Boys worry more than girls about vocation ("That I might not get a good job") and about acts of aggression or violence ("Getting beat up at school," "That I might kill myself," "Physical abuse by a parent," and "Nuclear bombing of the U.S."). These findings appear to reflect a certain degree of socialization to traditional sex-role expectations.

WORRIES: YOUTH SELF-REPORTS COMPARED WITH PARENTS' ESTIMATES

How much do parents know about the worries of their children? To address this question, we asked parents to respond to fifteen of the worry questions "as you think your child will." The questions are listed below in the form and sequence in which they appeared in the survey. Figures listed following the item display the discrepancy between parents' estimates and their child's response. Specifically, parents were given these instructions:

Your child's survey includes this next section. In this section your child will tell how much he or she worries about different things. *Fill out this section as you think your child will.*

> Very much
> Quite a bit
> Somewhat
> Very little
> Not at all

Remember: Imagine you are your child as you answer. Answer these questions as you think he or she would. If you are not sure, just make your best guess. I *(meaning your child)* worry . . .

· About how my friends treat me (Figure 17)
· That I might kill myself
· That someone might force me to do sexual things I don't want to do (Figure 15)
· About how well other kids like me (Figure 18)
· That one of my parents will hit me so hard that I will be badly hurt
· That I may die soon
· That a nuclear bomb might be dropped on America (Figure 16)
· That one of my parents might die
· About all the people who are hungry and poor in our country (Figure 13)
· That I might get beat up at school
· That one of my parents might stop loving me if I disappoint them
· About how much my mother or father drinks
· About all the drugs and drinking I see around me (Figure 12)
· About how I'm doing in school
· About my looks
· About all the violence that happens in our country (Figure 14)

Only youth who had both a mother and a father participating in the survey were included in this analysis, giving us a pool of about 3,700 matched triplicates (child/mother/father). Several important findings emerge:

· Parents radically *under*estimate the extent to which young adolescents worry about potentially hazardous or destructive events and forces. Youth report much more worry about these than parents perceive or admit.
· Parents' estimates are particularly discrepant for worries about hunger and poverty and about violence, and these estimates tend to be more discrepant for fifth and sixth graders than for older youth.
· Parents *over*estimate the extent to which youth worry about peer relationships.
· Mothers tend to estimate youth worries with no greater accuracy than fathers.

SUMMARY AND IMPLICATIONS

Young adolescents appear to have a number of concerns that parents do not fully recognize or understand. Parents may find that concerted efforts to discuss these issues will lead to a strengthening of the parent-child relationship.

Some worries expressed by young adolescents—sexual abuse, parent death, divorce—are delicate subjects. Schools and other youth-serving organizations should consider developing resources to help parents find effective ways to broach these topics with their children. In the case of sexual abuse, organizations might help young adolescents develop skills for dealing with sexually abusive adults.

Fifth- and sixth-grade youth are not as immune to "real world" concerns as some would hope. A sizable percentage of young adolescents have a deep concern about nuclear war. It is likely that this concern will continue to grow and that more youth will come to share it. They need some forum in which they can express and explore these and other concerns with adult guidance.

Fifth-grade youth report a high degree of concern about hunger and poverty. This sensitivity appears to decrease with age, perhaps because fifth graders lack structured opportunities to translate this concern into meaningful action. One way in which schools, churches, and other youth-serving organizations can best help young people deal with these worries is by finding ways for them to participate in working toward solution of the problems.

Figure 12   Worry About Drugs and Alcohol: Youth Compared with Parents' Estimates

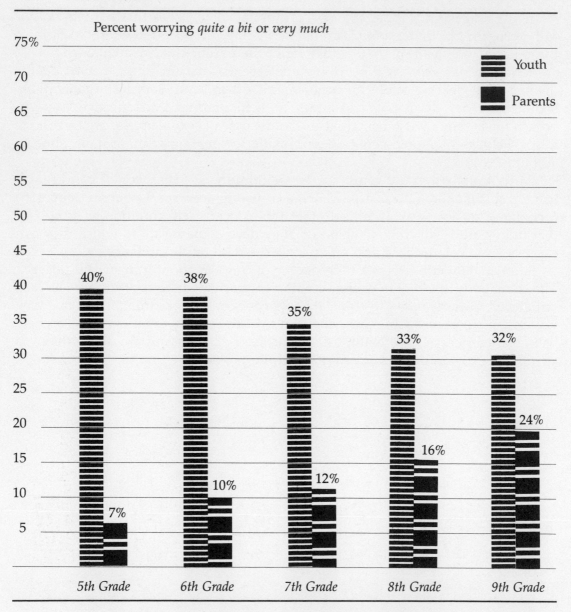

Percent worrying *quite a bit* or *very much*

How much do you worry about "all the drugs and drinking I see around me"?

How much do you think your child worries about "all the drugs and drinking I see around me"?

Figure 13   Worry About Hunger and Poverty: Youth Compared with Parents' Estimates

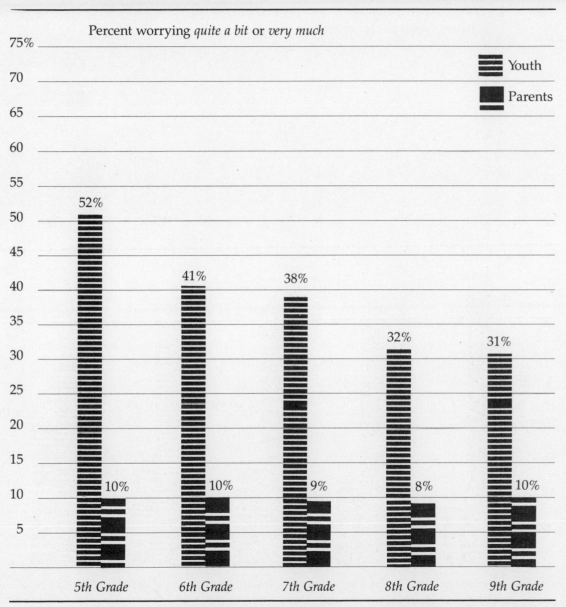

Percent worrying *quite a bit* or *very much*

How much do you worry about all the people who are hungry and poor in our country?

How much do you think your child worries about all the people who are hungry and poor in our country?

Figure 14 Worry About Violence in America: Youth Compared with Parents' Estimates

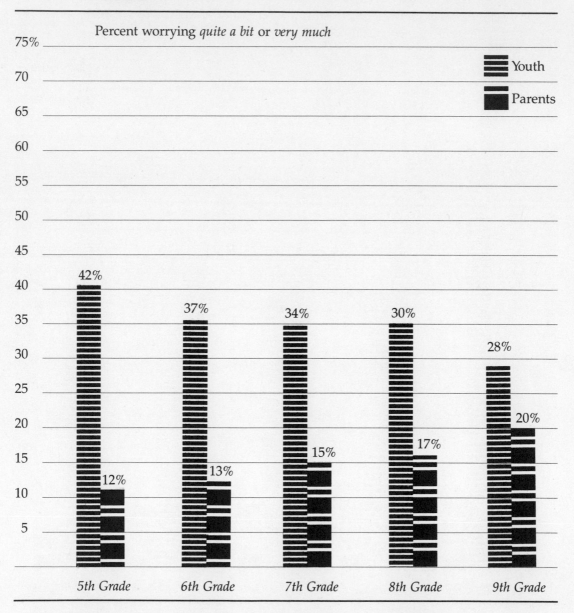

How much do you worry about all the violence that happens in our country?

How much do you think your child worries about all the violence that happens in our country?

Figure 15   Worry About Sexual Abuse: Youth Compared with Parents' Estimates

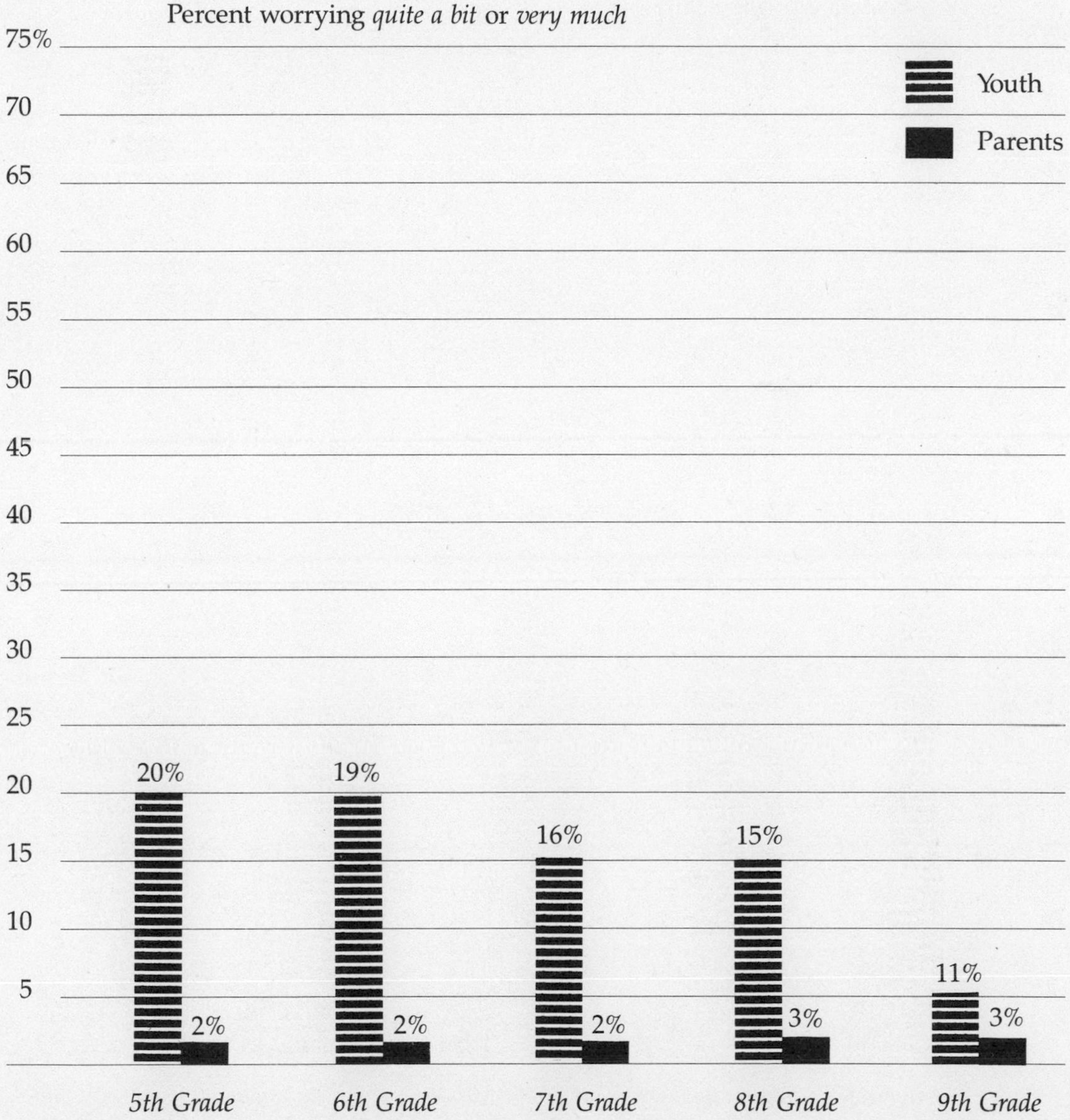

Percent worrying *quite a bit* or *very much*

How much do you worry that "someone might force me to do sexual things I don't want to do"?

How much do you think your child worries that "someone might force me to do sexual things I don't want to do"?

Figure 16 Worry About Nuclear War: Youth Compared with Parents' Estimates

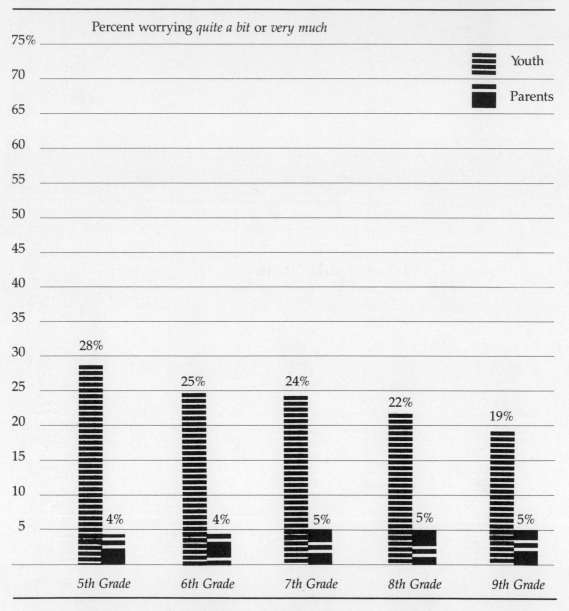

How much do you worry that a nuclear bomb might be dropped on America?

How much do you think your child worries that a nuclear bomb might be dropped on America?

Figure 17 Worry About "How My Friends Treat Me": Youth Compared with Parents' Estimates

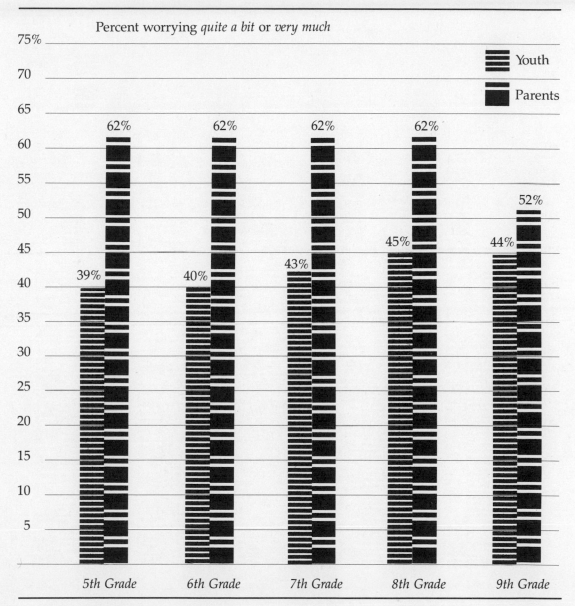

Percent worrying *quite a bit* or *very much*

How much do you worry about "how my friends treat me"?

How much do you think your child worries about "how my friends treat me"?

Figure 18   Worry About Being Liked by Others: Youth Compared with Parents' Estimates

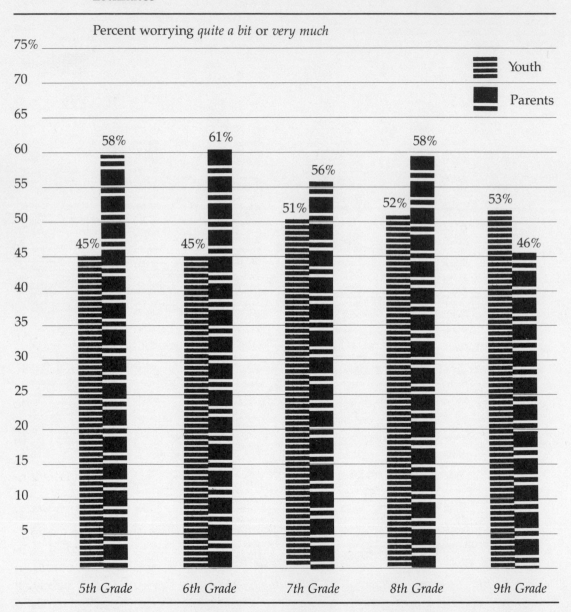

Percent worrying *quite a bit* or *very much*

How much do you worry about "how well other kids like me"?

How much do you think your child worries about "how well other kids like me"?

CHAPTER 5

Questions of Right and Wrong

- **In all five grades, more than 80 percent judge the following actions to be wrong: disturbing the classroom, shoplifting, and racial discrimination.**
- **Between the fifth and ninth grades, the perceived wrongness of lying to parents and of thirteen-year-olds drinking alcohol decreases.**
- **Girls are more likely than boys to attribute wrongness to each of the six behaviors explored in this chapter.**

One of the nearly universal goals of parents is to transmit to their children a firm set of moral values and beliefs. To accomplish this goal they employ a variety of techniques, including rewarding "good" behavior, admonishing "bad" behavior, and pointing out what is "good" and "bad" in the behavior of others. Parents have traditionally looked to schools, churches, and youth programs to cooperate in their efforts to teach moral beliefs.

Schools, churches, and other institutions that relate to young people do in fact cooperate in the attempt to inculcate a set of moral standards in young people, even though no formal identification or communication of these standards exists. Such standards are implemented, in part, simply in order to make life livable in group settings. Adults in most group settings discourage tardiness, encourage the taking of responsibility, encourage telling the truth, and discourage young adolescents' consumption of alcohol and use of other chemical substances. They encourage respect for property and for the feelings of others. In common with parents, they try to influence young people toward "good" behavior.

Most people assume that our behaviors are dictated by our beliefs. A child who believes, for example, that cheating is wrong will not cheat, or so the reasoning goes. Although it is a reasonable and common premise, the jury is still out as to whether the assumption is correct. Many psychologists and moral educators view moral development as being much more complicated than most of us think. Some authorities argue that moral behavior is dictated more by situational factors (for example, the rewards or punishments that will occur after the action or the likelihood that one's behavior will be seen by someone else) than by beliefs or values that one holds.[1]

Other experts describe the application of beliefs and values to real situations as a complex cognitive task, requiring a person to first make the connection between an abstract, general principle and a particular action and then to monitor the behavior, reflecting on its consistency or inconsistency with one's belief premises. Whether or not young adolescents have attained the cognitive sophistication it takes to handle such a complex task is still open to question. We associate Lawrence Kohlberg and others with yet another view of moral development. This approach suggests that a person's moral orientation cannot be directly taught. Rather, it is something we create for ourselves based upon our ability to reason and our experience "in the real world."[2]

What this all shows is that the process of moral development is extremely complex. Neither scholars nor practitioners can agree on exactly what determines healthy, positive moral development. To muddy the waters even more, people hold a wide variety of opinions about what "moral" means. To some, morality means abiding by widely shared social norms (for example, telling the truth, being honest, not picking on little kids). To others, the moral imperative is to love, that is, to be kind, helpful, compassionate, concerned about people. To still others, being moral means committing oneself to social causes such as justice or world peace.

As we raise here a topic surrounded by so much complexity, we do not pretend to offer answers about the best way to further moral education or about precisely what "right" is in all situations. What we can do is to report what young adolescents say they believe to be right and wrong. This overview of moral beliefs yields baseline information useful for evaluating how well certain moral messages are being caught.

The survey asked young adolescents about six moral issues. Four of them deal with areas of great concern to educators and parents alike: respect for authority, stealing, lying, and use of alcohol. The other two—abortion and racial prejudice—though perhaps not as universally discussed are also important.

The survey presented the subject as follows on the next page:

For each situation given below, decide how right or wrong you think it is. A reminder: answer honestly what *you* think. Your response choices are

VR   Very right
R   Right
NS   Not sure
W   Wrong
VW   Very wrong

1. You are in one of your classes at school. The teacher is trying to get all the kids to quit talking and running around so the class can learn something. Some kids ignore the teacher and keep on fooling around. How right or wrong are they?
2. Tracy thinks that shoplifting from a big store is not so bad because "they'll never miss it." She steals a $25 radio from a large department store. How right or wrong is it for her to steal the radio?
3. Gary is 12. His parents expect him to do his homework. Sometimes he lies to his parents and tells them he has done his homework when he really hasn't. He does this so that his parents won't keep asking him about his homework. How right or wrong is Gary to lie to his parents?
4. Jim is 13. Sometimes he and his friends get together and drink a couple of cans of beer. How right or wrong are they to do this?
5. Alice, who is 15, didn't think she would get pregnant, but the doctor said she was. She decided she did not want to have the baby, so she went to another doctor and had an abortion (an operation to get rid of it). How right or wrong was it for her to have this abortion?
6. The Olsons are a white family who live in a neighborhood of mostly white people. A black family is considering buying a house nearby. The Olsons are trying to stop the black family from moving in. How right or wrong is it for the Olsons to do this?

GRADE DIFFERENCES

Table 5.1 gives percentages of response to the survey situations.

Three of the actions are judged wrong by more than 80 percent in each of the five grades. These are: disrupting a classroom, shoplifting, and racial discrimination.

Table 5.1   Grade Differences in Moral Beliefs

	5th	6th	7th	8th	9th	Total
Disrupting classroom						
Wrong or very wrong	82%	84%	84%	87%	86%	85%
Not sure	7%	7%	8%	7%	7%	7%
Right or very right	11%	9%	8%	6%	7%	8%
Shoplifting						
Wrong or very wrong	89%	91%	92%	93%	91%	92%
Not sure	4%	3%	3%	3%	3%	3%
Right or very right	7%	6%	5%	4%	6%	5%
Lying to parents						
Wrong or very wrong	87%	87%	82%	80%	75%	82%
Not sure	6%	8%	11%	13%	17%	11%
Right or very right	7%	5%	7%	7%	8%	7%
Drinking alcohol at age 13						
Wrong or very wrong	81%	81%	78%	72%	66%	76%
Not sure	12%	13%	15%	21%	23%	17%
Right or very right	7%	6%	7%	8%	11%	8%
Abortion at age 15						
Wrong or very wrong	36%	45%	47%	51%	49%	46%
Not sure	48%	41%	39%	35%	34%	39%
Right or very right	16%	14%	14%	14%	17%	15%
Racial discrimination						
Wrong or very wrong	84%	86%	86%	87%	86%	86%
Not sure	8%	9%	8%	7%	8%	8%
Right or very right	8%	5%	6%	6%	6%	6%

Two actions decrease in perceived "wrongness" with an increase in grade: lying to parents as wrong drops from 87 percent in fifth grade to 75 percent in ninth grade. Drinking alcohol at thirteen is perceived as wrong by 81 percent of fifth graders but decreases to 66 percent of ninth graders. Even though the preceived wrongness of these two actions decreases, the majority of ninth graders still claim the action is wrong.

"Abortion at age 15" is a special case. The percentage of young adolescents who judge it wrong is much lower than for any of the other actions. On the other five cases the lowest "wrongness" is 61 percent (the response figure for ninth-grade boys on alcohol use); on abortion the highest figure is 54 percent.

Many of the youth in this study may not know what the term *abortion* means, or if they do know what it means, they may have had insufficient opportunity to discuss the issue and come to a clear position on its rightness or wrongness. In any case, their lack of certainty is evident in the large percentage who report "not sure" to this question.

SEX DIFFERENCES

Figures 19–24 show how boys and girls responded to the six questions. some major findings are these:

· On five of the six issues, more girls than boys respond "wrong" or "very wrong" at every grade.
· The single exception is the issue of abortion, on which girls and boys respond almost exactly alike until the eighth and ninth grades. At these grade levels, girls again attribute greater "wrongness" to the behavior than do boys.
· Thirty comparisons (six questions times five grades) of boys and girls occur in these tables. A sex difference occurs on twenty-seven of them. In all twenty-seven cases girls report greater "wrongness" than boys.

SUMMARY

What, now, do we know about the moral beliefs of young adolescents? We know that, to a considerable extent, they share certain standards and, further, that youth more commonly affirm certain behaviors to be wrong than many adults may have surmised.

But do their opinions about behavior match their actions? The survey included three situations involving lying, shoplifting, and drinking alcohol. When we examine the relationship of young people's moral belief about an action and their own behavior, we find that what most people would hope is indeed so: the more wrong a young adolescent judges an action to be, the less likely he or she is to report actually engaging in that behavior.[3] This is an important finding and an encouraging one.

A caution must be attached to this finding. Although we know that beliefs about lying, shoplifting, and drinking alcohol are statistically linked to the incidence of the behaviors themselves, we do not know how. Which causes which? Do young people refrain from shoplifting because they consider it wrong? In that case we could say that belief affects behavior. Or do some young people shoplift and then persuade themselves that it is not wrong as a way of managing their guilt? In that case we would have to acknowledge that behavior affects belief. As it is, we know only that the beliefs and the behaviors are connected, allowing us to see into an important corner of young adolescents' lives and to find that their behaviors tend to be congruent with their moral beliefs.

Figure 19   Belief About Disrupting Classroom

You are in one of your classes at school. The teacher is trying to get all the kids to quit talking and running around so the class can learn something. Some kids ignore the teacher and keep on fooling around. How right or wrong are they?

Figure 20 Belief About Shoplifting

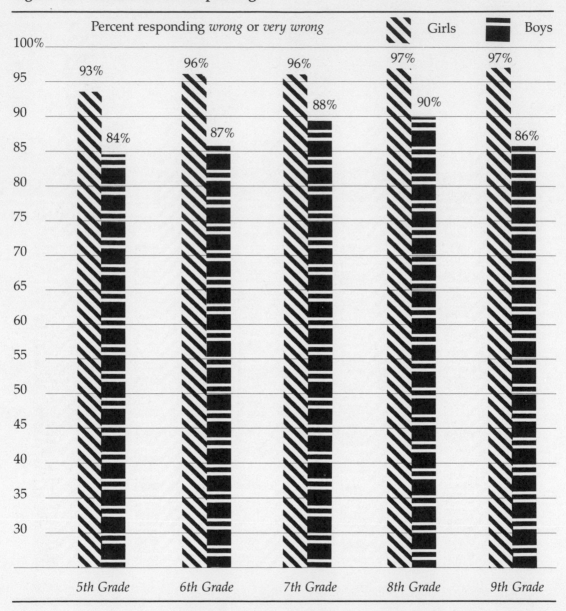

Tracy thinks that shoplifting from a big store is not so bad because "they'll never miss it." She steals a $25 radio from a large department store. How right or wrong is it for her to steal the radio?

Figure 21   Belief About Lying to Parents

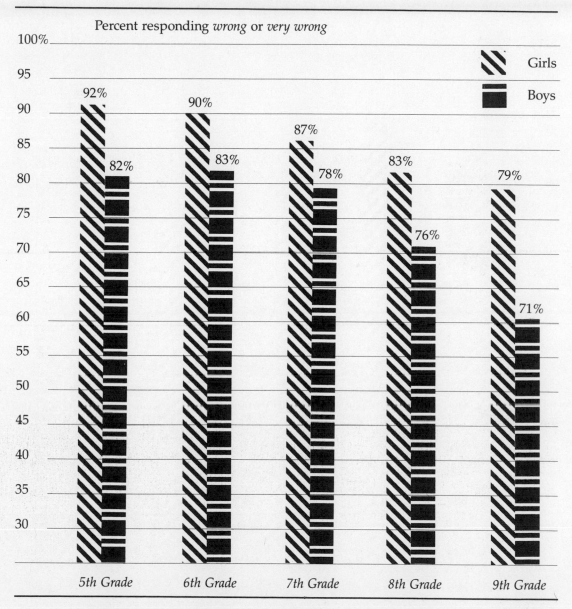

Percent responding *wrong* or *very wrong*

Gary is 12. His parents expect him to do his homework. Sometimes he lies to his parents and tells them he has done his homework when he really hasn't. He does this so that his parents won't keep asking him about his homework. How right or wrong is Gary to lie to his parents?

Figure 22 Belief About Drinking Alcohol

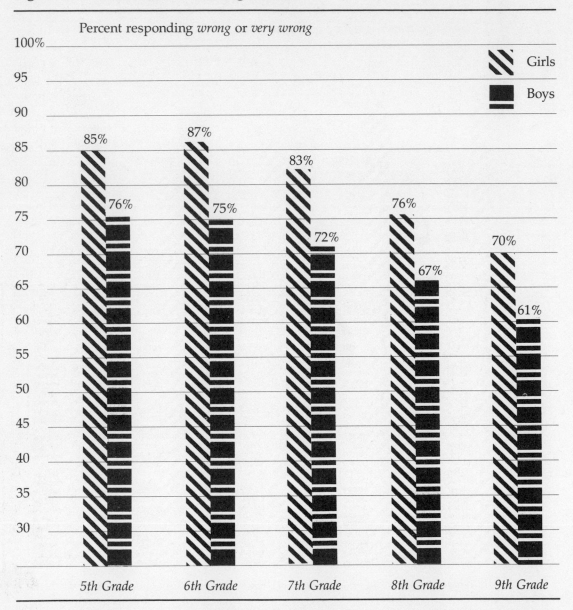

Percent responding *wrong* or *very wrong*

Jim is 13. Sometimes he and his friends get together and drink a couple of cans of beer. How right or wrong are they to do this?

Figure 23   Belief About Abortion

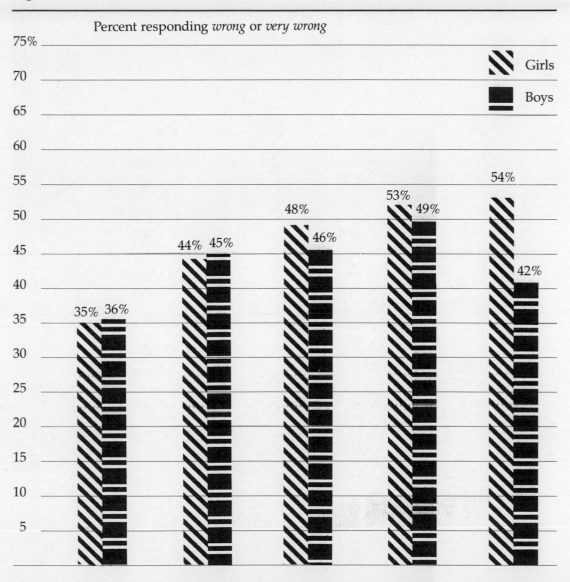

Percent responding *wrong* or *very wrong*

Alice, who is 15, didn't think she would get pregnant, but the doctor said she was. She decided she did not want to have the baby, so she went to another doctor and had an abortion (an operation to get rid of it). How right or wrong was it for her to have this abortion?

Figure 24   Belief About Racial Discrimination

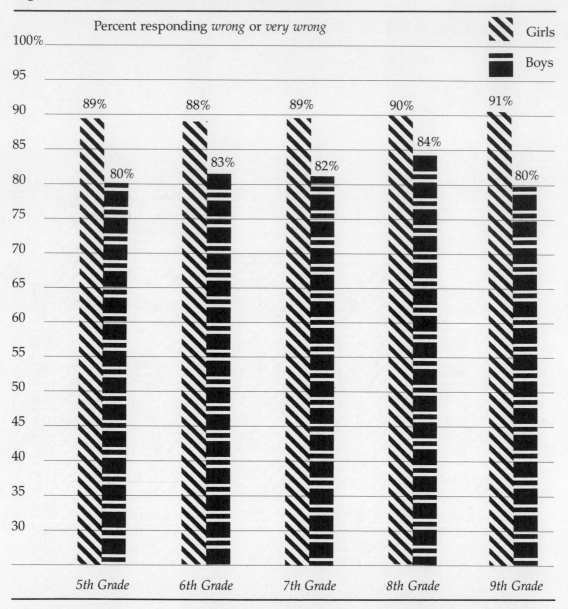

The Olsons are a white family who live in a neighborhood of mostly white people. A black family is considering buying a house nearby. The Olsons are trying to stop the black family from moving in. How right or wrong is it for the Olsons to do this?

CHAPTER 6

Values: What's Important in Life?

- · The two life goals most important to young adolescents in each grade between fifth and ninth are "to have a happy family life" and "to get a good job when I am older."
- · The two values that increase the most in importance between fifth and ninth grade are "to make my own decisions" and "to do something important with my life."
- · Values that decrease in importance between fifth and ninth grade include God, church, and concern for people and the world.
- · Girls are more likely than boys to embrace values of friendship, family, and concerns for people and the world.
- · Boys are more likely than girls to hold hedonistic values.

The values of young adolescents can be easily misread. Judging from what one observes of their behavior in groups—noisy, pushing, shoving, impulsive—one would conclude that most of them value whatever is quick, loud, self-aggrandizing, and spectacular.

But young people, sometimes even more successfully than adults, hide much of what is real about themselves. The noisy show distracts the observer from some values that might come as a surprise and that contradict the image the young person presents. In a sense, values tell us what people are reaching for rather than who they now are. The way people behave in the present may be quite discrepant with their dreams and goals.

Our survey presented young adolescents with a list of twenty-four values. It asked them the following:

What are the things you want in life? Listed below are things that some people want. Read through the entire list without making any marks. Then go through the list again and decide *how much you want* each one. Here are your choices:

VL *Very little or not at all*—I don't want this much at all
S *Somewhat*—I want this somewhat
Q *Quite a bit*—I want this quite a bit
VM *Very much*—I want this very much
T *At the top of the list*—this is one of the 3 or 4 things I want most in life

· To be good in music, drama, or art
· To have a happy family life
· To make my parents proud of me
· To make my own decisions
· To do things that help people
· To feel safe and secure in my neighborhood
· To feel good about myself
· To be popular at school
· To have lots of fun and good times
· To understand my feelings
· To have lots of money
· To have God at the center of my life
· To have a world without hunger or poverty
· To get a good job when I am older
· To have things (such as clothes, records, etc.) as nice as other kids have
· To do something important with my life
· To do well in school
· To have a world without war
· To be really good at sports
· To be different in some way from all other kids I know
· To have friends I can count on
· To do whatever I want to do, when I want to do it
· To be part of a church or synagogue
· To have clothes and hair that look good to other kids

A key question in a survey like this is whether or not we can trust the information given. Will respondents be tempted to give "motherhood and apple pie" answers, the kinds of replies they think adults want to hear? While some may do so, two pieces of evidence in particular suggest that the trends we find in young adolescents' expressed values are bona fide. First, the patterns of responses are consistent with what we find in other parts of the survey. If, for example, a young adolescent places high value on friends, we find that same adolescent emphasizing friendship concerns in Chapter 4 and claiming high peer influence in Chapter 2. Secondly, we find agreement between parents' descriptions of young adolescents and what young adolescents say about themselves.[1] Hence, there is corroborative evidence that the data on young adolescents' values reflect what is really important to them.

Table 6.1 lists in descending order the percentage of eight thousand young adolescents who said that each of these values was of high importance to them, responding either "I want this very much" or "at the top of the list."

Table 6.2 shows the overall averages for the twenty-four items and also notes items that increase or decrease in value between fifth and ninth grade.[2] From this table we see that nine values remain consistent throughout the years of early adolescence.

When we combine the two lists, "to have a happy family life" and "to get a good job when I am older" rank as the top values for this age group, outranking what one might consider more probable values, such as friends, freedom, and school. Over 80 percent of all young adolescents put these two values at the top of their lists or indicated that they wanted them very much. (Slight discrepancies occur between the two lists because the first takes into account only those who ranked the values very high. When the scores of all youth are taken into account, the ranking shifts slightly.)

Table 6.1 What's Important in Life?

Percent saying want very much *or* at the top of my list

To get a good job	84%
To have a happy family life	82%
To do well in school	82%
To do something important	80%
To make my parents proud	80%
To have friends I can count on	80%
A world without war	77%
To feel good about myself	76%
A world without hunger	70%
Lots of fun and good times	69%
God at center of my life	66%
To have a safe neighborhood	64%
To understand my feelings	57%
To be part of a church	55%
To make my own decisions	53%
To be good at sports	53%
To do things that help people	52%
To look good to other kids	52%
To have nice things	50%
To be popular at school	46%
To have lots of money	42%
To be different from other kids	35%
To be good in music, drama, art	35%
To do what I want to do	30%

Table 6.2   Relationship of Values to Grade in School

Value	RANK All Youth	Average of All Youth (1 = low, 5 = high)	Increase from 5th to 9th	Decrease from 5th to 9th
To have a happy family life	1	4.24		
To get a good job	2	4.16	+.17	
To do something important	3	4.10	+.25	
To do well in school	4	4.09		−.09
To make my parents proud	5	4.06		
A world without war	6	4.00		−.21
To have friends I can count on	7	3.99	+.13	
To feel good about myself	8	3.97	+.15	
God at center of my life	9	3.89		−.24
Lots of fun and good times	10	3.81		
A world without hunger	11	3.80		
To have a safe neighborhood	12	3.68		−.23
To understand my feelings	13	3.56		
To make my own decisions	14	3.51	+.49	
To be part of a church	15	3.49		−.18
To do things that help people	16	3.48		−.16
To be good at sports	17	3.44		−.19
To look good to other kids	18	3.41		
To have nice things	19	3.39		
To be popular at school	20	3.28	+.19	
To have lots of money	21	3.23		
To be different from other kids	22	2.95		
To do what I want to do	23	2.85	+.13	
To be good in music, drama, art	24	2.79		−.26

Friends and school rank near the top of the list, along with family and vocation. The two religious values, "to have God at the center of my life" and "to be part of a church," are located toward the middle of the value hierarchy. Young adolescents report strong global concerns even though the rank declines slightly as they grow older. Nevertheless, overall, "to have a world without war" is sixth and seventh on the lists and "to have a world without hunger or poverty" is ninth and eleventh.

Toward the bottom of the list are values related to materialism ("to have lots of money," "to have things as nice as other kids have"). The value attaining the lowest average of all is "to be good in music, drama, or art."

Seven of the twenty-four values become more important as young adolescents move from fifth to ninth grade. These reflect, in general, youth's growing separateness from family, their individuality, and their need to "make it" on their own in the adult world. The value that increases most (twenty percentage points) between fifth and ninth grade is "to make my own decisions." (See Figure 4.)

Eight of the twenty-four values become less important between fifth and ninth grades. These eight include values having to do with church, school, and helping people. Figure 25 shows the decrease in young adolescents' value placed on God and the church.

VALUE THEMES

To form a more cohesive picture of young adolescents' value development, we merged the twenty-four values into nine themes or orientations. These are organized as follows:[3]

1. **Friendship**
   To have friends I can count on
2. **Autonomy**
   To make my own decisions
3. **Future achievement**
   To do something important with my life
   To get a good job when I am older
4. **Family**
   To have a happy family life
   To make my parents proud of me
5. **Peer acceptance**
   To be popular at school
   To have things as nice as other kids have
   To have clothes and hair that look good to other kids

Figure 25   Value Placed on God and Church

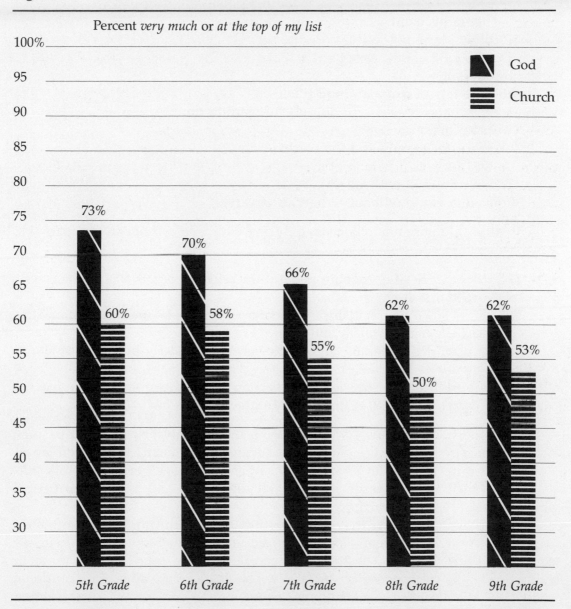

Percent *very much* or *at the top of my list*

How much do you want "to have God at the center of my life"?
How much do you want "to be part of a church or synagogue"?

6. **Institutional connection**
   To do well in school
   To be part of a church
7. **Self-enhancement**
   To understand my feelings
   To feel good about myself
8. **Hedonism**
   To have lots of fun and good times
   To do whatever I want to do, when I want to do it
   To have lots of money
9. **Concern for people and the world**
   To do things that help people
   To have a world without war
   To have a world without hunger or poverty

The nine value orientations change during early adolescence in the following ways:[4]

· The importance of autonomy and future achievement *strongly increase* between fifth and ninth grades.
· The importance of friendship, self-enhancement, and peer acceptance *increase slightly* between fifth and ninth grades.
· The importance of family and hedonism *remain stable* between fifth and ninth grades.
· The importance of institutional connection and concern for people and the world *decrease* between fifth and ninth grades.

During early adolescence, youth become increasingly self-oriented as they prepare to assume adult roles. Autonomy, future achievement, and self-enhancement are components of an emphasis on individual development. As this self-orientation increases, however, institutional connection and concern for people and the world tend to decrease.

In Chapter 2 we noted that between fifth and ninth grade peer influence increases, yet ties to parents continue to be important. Our findings here are consistent with that. We see that peer acceptance and friendship increase in value but not at the expense of the family. The decreasing value of institutional connection also confirms the findings about church and school discussed in Chapter 2.

SEX DIFFERENCES IN VALUES

Table 6.3 shows how boys and girls compare on each of the twenty-four value items.[5] A major finding is the comparability of boys and girls on the rank order of values. The similarity is rather remarkable. The only value that differs dramatically in its positioning is "to be good at sports." This value ranks twelfth for boys, but twentieth for girls. Only three other values are of higher importance to boys than to girls: "to have lots of money," "to do whatever I want to do, when I want to do it," and "to be different in some way from other kids I know."

Table 6.3   Sex Differences in Values

Value	Average For All Girls	Average For All Boys	Rank For Girls	Rank For Boys
To have a happy family life	4.32*	4.11	1	2
To get a good job	4.19*	4.11	2	1
To do something important	4.19*	3.99	3	3
To do well in school	4.17*	3.99	4	4
To make my parents proud	4.13*	3.97	5	5
A world without war	4.10*	3.88	6	7
To have friends I can count on	4.07*	3.91	7	6
To feel good about myself	4.03*	3.87	8	8
God at center of my life	3.97*	3.85	9	9
Lots of fun and good times	3.86*	3.73	11	10
A world without hunger	3.88*	3.71	10	11
To have a safe neighborhood	3.74*	3.61	12	13
To understand my feelings	3.63*	3.49	13	15
To make my own decisions	3.58*	3.43	14	16
To be part of a church	3.50	3.49	16	14
To do things that help people	3.56*	3.38	15	18
To be good at sports	3.25	3.69*	20	12
To look good to other kids	3.46*	3.35	17	20
To have nice things	3.41	3.38	18	17
To be popular at school	3.28	3.29	19	21
To have lots of money	3.10	3.36*	21	19
To be different from other kids	2.90	3.00*	23	22
To do what I want to do	2.74	2.94*	24	23
To be good in music, drama, art	3.00*	2.55	22	24

* Indicates which sex has a significantly higher average

Girls rank seventeen of the values higher than boys. The three on which girls are most different from boys are: "to be good in music, drama, or art," "to have a happy family life," and "to have friends I can count on." (Figure 26 compares girls and boys on the latter value.)

Boys and girls agree in their ranking of these three values: "to make my own decisions," "to be popular," and "to have things as nice as other kids have." On a fourth, "to get a good job when I am older," shown in Figure 27, boys' ranking catches up to girls' by the ninth grade.

Using the nine value orientations described earlier, we summarize here the similarities and differences.[6]

Value orientations on which girls are higher:
> Friendship
> Family
> Concern for people and the world
> Institutional connection
> Future achievement
> Self-enhancement

Value orientations on which boys are higher:
> Hedonism

Value orientations on which there is no sex difference:
> Autonomy
> Peer acceptance

Four of the nine value orientations are communal or relational in which the focus is on one's ties to other people. Girls rank three of the four—friendship, family, and concern for people and the world—higher than boys do. In valuing peer acceptance, the fourth relational value orientation, boys and girls do not differ. Four other orientations place the focus on the self. These are hedonism, future achievement, self-enhancement, and autonomy. Boys' rankings are higher on hedonism, and girls' are higher on achievement and self-enhancement.

Other researchers have argued that males tend to rank self-oriented values higher and females tend to rank communal values higher.[7] We find things not quite that simple. To be sure, girls rank communal values higher than boys. But for self-oriented values, girls' rankings are higher on two. We may be seeing here a cultural change in which options and opportunities for girls are expanding. Accordingly, we now see girls embracing not only communal values but also values that strengthen and bolster the self.

Some interesting correlates appear with young adolescents' value orientations. We find that boys and girls with hedonistic values tend to have been exposed to more mass media than youth with less hedonistic values. To conclude

Figure 26   Sex Differences in Value Placed on Friendship

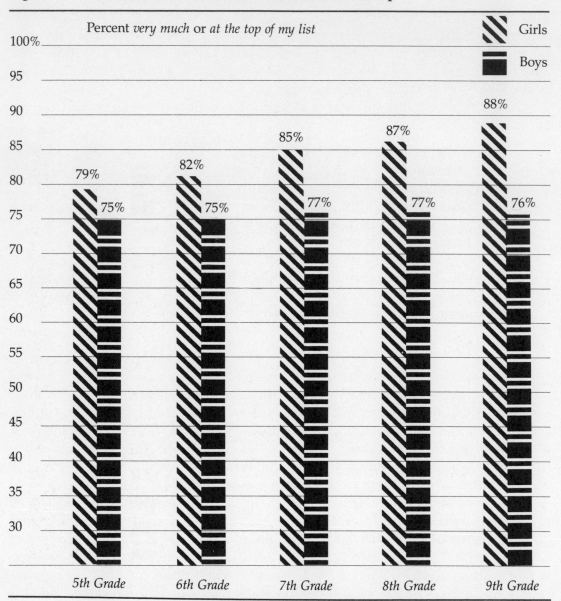

How much do you want "to have friends I can count on"?

Figure 27   Sex Differences in Value Placed on Getting a Good Job

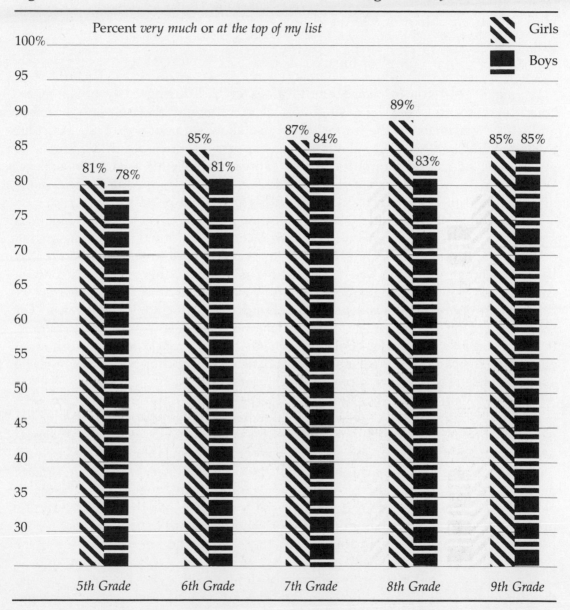

Percent *very much* or *at the top of my list*

Girls

Boys

5th Grade — 81% / 78%
6th Grade — 85% / 81%
7th Grade — 87% / 84%
8th Grade — 89% / 83%
9th Grade — 85% / 85%

How much do you want "to get a good job when I am older"?

that the mass media teach and reward this value orientation may be premature but nonetheless is a reasonable possibility. On the more positive side, one of the main features of young adolescents who rank concern for people and the world high is a strong connection to the church.[8]

SUMMARY AND IMPLICATIONS

A major shift toward some adult values occurs during early adolescence. Young adolescents show increasing interest in autonomy and self-enhancement and a stronger focus on the future. They also show signs of a growing need for responsibility and meaningful work. We encourage educators and parents to give young adolescents opportunity to express these values as they emerge. Work with young adolescents should include structured opportunities to make decisions and to engage in tasks that adults consider important.

The interest of young adolescents in getting "a good job when I am older" is something of a surprise. We do not know whether or not this interest among fifth- through ninth-grade youth is actually something new. Prior to World War II, when higher education was not accessible as it is now, this vocational concern could be expected. But many observers have believed that in the last twenty or thirty years job concerns are usually delayed until later adolescent years. For whatever reasons, young adolescents show a high interest in future occupation. It may be that what young adolescents want now is not so much information about specific careers but a sense of confidence that good opportunities will be available when they have completed their formal education.

We find that, at this age, increased value on self-determination and self-expression accompanies a decreased value on helping people and on global issues of hunger and peace. Of course we would prefer to see youth become more self-reliant and individualistic *and* hold on to important communal values. Parents and youth agencies might try to help young adolescents meet their rising needs for responsibility and industry by engaging them in meaningful projects aimed at communal issues, oriented to the well-being of others (for example, hunger relief, environmental protection, or volunteer work in projects that would put the young adolescent in touch with the elderly, the very young, or those with handicapping conditions).

Though boys and girls are surprisingly similar in the way they rank values, the differences we discover between them are important. As we saw in earlier chapters, we now see again that a number of the more desirable qualities are more evident in girls than in boys. In this chapter, we see girls striking a better balance than boys between individualistic and communal values. In Chapter 3, we noted that girls are more likely than boys to attain a balance of masculine and feminine sex-roles. Perhaps girls during the fifth through ninth grades are a year or two ahead of boys in social and emotional maturity as well as in biological maturity.

CHAPTER 7

Social Attitudes:
Prejudices, Political Perspectives

· Only a minority of young adolescents show prejudice on the basis of race, sex, or age.
· Racial prejudice decreases slightly between the fifth and ninth grades.
· Prejudiced young adolescents tend to have prejudiced parents.
· Most young adolescents oppose increased government spending for weapons.
· Most young adolescents favor increased government efforts to combat poverty and hunger.

In this chapter, we briefly look at the stand of young adolescents on such social issues as race, the rights and roles of women and the aged, and politics.

RACE

We found little evidence of racial prejudice in this group. Only a small minority of young adolescents agree with the two statements listed below.

	5th	6th	7th	8th	9th
It is wrong for a boy and girl of different races to date each other.					
Percent who "agree" or "strongly agree"	17	16	15	16	18
I don't trust people of other races.					
Percent who "agree" or "strongly agree"	14	13	9	8	9

Similarly, as we saw in Chapter 5, only a small minority of young adolescents believe it is morally permissible for whites to resist the racial integration of their neighborhoods. Here are their responses to that issue.

	5th	6th	7th	8th	9th
The Olsons are a white family who live in a neighborhood of mostly white people. A black family is considering buying a house nearby. The Olsons are trying to stop the black family from moving in. How right or wrong is it for the Olsons to do this?					
Percent who answer "right" or "very right"	7	5	6	5	6

We can see that, generally speaking, prejudice is low and decreases slightly between the fifth and ninth grades. Furthermore, girls report less prejudice than boys.[1]

WOMEN

The majority of young adolescents take an egalitarian position on men and women. Only a minority seem to favor men over women, as the following percentages show:

	5th	6th	7th	8th	9th
I think the father should make all the important decisions in a family.					
Percent who "agree" or "strongly agree"					
Boys	34	35	28	28	32
Girls	28	26	23	18	17
I think women should have all the same rights as men.					
Percent who "disagree" or "strongly disagree"					
Boys	20	20	23	22	27
Girls	7	7	7	11	18
I think that when a girl gets pregnant, it is more her fault than the boy's.					
Percent who "agree" or "strongly agree"					
Boys	19	17	20	16	18
Girls	15	16	19	16	16

	5th	6th	7th	8th	9th
I think men should have more freedom than women.					
Percent who "agree" or "strongly agree"					
Boys	17	15	17	16	15
Girls	4	3	2	3	4

In general, across these four questions, the difference between boys and girls stays relatively constant across the five grades.[2] On the matter of responsibility for pregnancy, boys and girls have similar views. On the three other statements, as might be expected, more boys than girls discriminate in favor of men.

ATTITUDES TOWARD OLDER PEOPLE

One survey item was designed to look at young adolescents' attitudes toward older adults. Responses to the statement, "I don't like to be around old people" are shown here.

	5th	6th	7th	8th	9th
I don't like to be around old people.					
Percent who say "somewhat true," "quite true" or "very true"					
Boys	21	21	27	28	32
Girls	17	17	18	19	17

More boys than girls agree with the statement. For boys, distaste for being around old people increases between fifth and ninth grade, where for girls there is little change.

RACISM, SEXISM, AND AGEISM—THE CONNECTION

Only a minority of young adolescents report a prejudice based on age, race, or sex. On all three, girls report less prejudice than boys. Grade level makes no apparent difference: racial prejudice declines a little between fifth and ninth grade, sexism stays stable, and dislike for older people increases, but only for boys.

We find that racism and sexism are tied to each other: if a young adolescent is racially prejudiced, he or she is also likely to have sexist attitudes. Both of these are strongly tied to parents' views on race and sex, suggesting that parental attitudes in these areas are transmitted to their children. Prejudice among young adolescents is usually higher in homes where parents exercise authoritarian control (that is, parents place high priority on obedience and permit no deviation from parental expectations). We could find no evidence that prejudice is related to either a young person's church involvement or religious certainty (see Chapter 8): young adolescents high on these two variables are just as likely to hold prejudiced views as those low on them.[3]

POLITICAL PERSPECTIVES

The development of political ideology is complex.[4] We did not attempt to probe this area deeply, but we did include two questions in order to get a rough approximation of political perspective. The first question is on the issue of government military spending. Here are young adolescents' responses.

	5th	6th	7th	8th	9th
Our country should spend more money for bombs and other weapons.					
Percent who "agree" or "strongly agree"					
Boys	17	18	18	20	21
Girls	4	6	5	5	5
Percent who "disagree" or "strongly disagree"					
Boys	60	59	60	58	56
Girls	72	68	72	71	73

Boys differ strongly from girls on this question, with more boys favoring spending for military weapons. However, the majority of both boys and girls disagree with the idea of increased government spending.

As shown below, a strong majority of young adolescents recommend that the government give increased attention to alleviating the suffering of people in need.

	5th	6th	7th	8th	9th
I think our government should do more to help people who are poor and hungry.					
Percent who "agree" or "strongly agree"					
Boys	88	88	86	81	75
Girls	91	90	90	84	83

Girls are slightly more positive toward government intervention than are boys. Support for government intervention tends to decrease with grade but never falls below three fourths of any group.

Opposition to increased government spending for military procurements and support for government involvement in social problems like poverty are usually recognized as aspects of a liberal political orientation. If so, the data presented here would suggest that the majority of young adolescents in this study tilt to the liberal side on these two issues. However, this conclusion may be premature. We do not know whether young adolescents are making informed judgments about government or are simply registering disapproval of war and poverty. Liberals and conservatives alike say they disapprove of war and poverty; they differ on the methods of dealing with these issues and the priority assigned to them. Our questions do not probe deeply enough into these realms to enable us to tell what philosophies undergird these young adolescents' responses.

CHAPTER 8

Religion: Importance, Beliefs, Themes

· **The majority of young adolescents report that religion is "the most important" or "one of the most important" influences in their lives.**
· **Boys attach less importance to religion than do girls.**
· **Young adolescents are more likely to experience religion as liberating than as restricting.**
· **Boys are more likely than girls to experience religion as restricting.**
· **Most young adolescents believe that religion has both *vertical* (focus on God) and *horizontal* (focus on acts of love and justice) responsibilities.**

Religion is a topic that has too often been downplayed or ignored in discussions of human development. Most textbooks on child and adolescent development pay relatively little attention to the role of religion. When these texts do pay attention to religion, the discussion often centers on cults and speculation as to why some adolescents are susceptible to this form of conversion experience. The reader receives the impression that religion is interesting as a human development issue only when it is expressed in a nontraditional form and is emotionally intense.

Religion deserves more serious treatment than that, if only because the vast majority of American children and adolescents are involved in some way with religion. Recent Gallup polls show that

· Seventy-four percent of thirteen- to fifteen-year-old youth say that religion is the most important or one of the most important influences in their lives.[1]
· Ninety-five percent of thirteen- to fifteen-year-old youth say they believe in "God or a universal spirit."[2]
· Sixty percent of American parents (of children under the age of eighteen) say that their children currently receive some form of religious instruction.[3] This 60 percent includes parents of teenagers and of infants. We could

reasonably expect the religious instruction figure to rise to 70 or 80 percent were it to include only ten- to fourteen-year-old children.

· Eighty-three percent of American adults say "they would want a child of theirs to receive religious instruction."[4]

Given this data, it is not unreasonable to claim that religion is a part of growing up in American society, a circumstance almost as universal as having parents or going to school.[5] The fact that the national organizations involved in this project have strong interest in religious development is one reason to include religion in this report. However, even if that were not the case, a chapter on religion clearly belongs in any report that claims to be a descriptive overview of child or adolescent development.

The nature of the thirteen participating national organizations does, of course, influence the data in this chapter. Because most of these groups are national church bodies, and because the more active youth within these organizations tended to participate in this study, we expect religion to be more important to some of the young adolescents in this study than it would be to other young adolescents in the general population. On the other hand, a sizable segment of the sample came from 4-H, which has no connection with the institutional church, and from the National Association of Homes for Children, which, though in part supported by church funding, places no conditions of church connection on the young people served. Another reason for including information on religious belief and practices for both adults and children stands out: we find that some significant behaviors and attitudes correlate more closely with religious belief and practice than with any other piece of data in the study. The changes in religion that occur between the fifth and ninth grades in this sample may well be the kinds of changes that would also appear in other samples of young adolescents.

THE IMPORTANCE OF RELIGION

As noted above, we should expect religion to be particularly valued by the young adolescents in this study. The responses to the following question show the extent of this interest.

	5th	6th	7th	8th	9th

Overall, how important is religion in your life?
   Percent who say, "the most important
   influence"

	5th	6th	7th	8th	9th
Boys	29	23	17	18	17
Girls	27	25	20	17	20

   Percent who say, "one of the most important
   influences"

Boys	31	31	32	31	29
Girls	33	32	35	38	35

   Percent who say, "a somewhat important
   influence"

Boys	29	36	36	38	36
Girls	29	35	37	37	34

   Percent who say, "one of the least important
   influences"

Boys	6	7	11	10	12
Girls	7	4	5	7	6

   Percent who say, "the least important
   influence"

Boys	4	3	4	4	6
Girls	4	2	4	2	4

Even though a majority of the young adolescents in this study are affiliated with the institutional church, they gave quite a range of responses on religious importance. Though the majority say religion is an important influence, about one third claim religion to be somewhat important, and another 10 to 15 percent say religion has very little importance to them.

Both boys and girls show a slight decline in religious importance between the fifth and ninth grades. This decline is most evident in the percentage who claim that religion is the "most important influence."

Some religious doubt evidently emerges during early adolescence, as shown by adolescents' responses to the following question:

	5th	6th	7th	8th	9th

I'm not sure what I believe about God.

	5th	6th	7th	8th	9th
Percent of boys who agree	45	46	51	55	62
Percent of girls who agree	42	46	52	53	54

The percentages of boys and girls who agree with the statement increases with grade, although the increase for boys is slightly greater. We can give a number of reasons why some initial doubt begins in these years. One has to do with cognitive development. As they begin to develop the capacity to engage in abstract reasoning, young people also begin to inquire why things are the way they are. They are able to entertain new possibilities and can see that things could be different. Inevitably, axioms of faith will be tested for their "reasonableness."

To chart the patterning of the importance of religion, we created an eight-item scale ranging from 1 (religion as peripheral) to 5 (religion as central). The averages for boys and girls in each of the five grades are shown in Figure 28. The trends for the two are quite different. Religious centrality is stable between fifth and ninth grade for girls. For boys, it begins a downward turn after sixth grade, with a particular drop between eighth and ninth grade.[6]

ORTHODOX BELIEFS

To discover that religion is or is not central provides one piece of information, but if religion is central, then the content of what is believed is especially important. To discover how near to traditional religious orthodoxy are the beliefs of young Protestants and Catholics (who comprised most of the sample), we inquired into three issues central to the Christian tradition: the existence of God, the identity of Jesus Christ, and the origins of the Bible. Their responses follow.

	5th	6th	7th	8th	9th	Total
Percent who agree with each of these statements about God:						
I know for sure that God exists.	62	63	62	61	59	62
I'm quite sure that God exists.	20	24	24	26	26	24
I'm not sure if God exists.	12	10	10	10	11	10
I don't think there is a God.	3	2	3	2	2	2
I know for sure that there is no such thing as God.	3	2	1	1	2	2

Figure 28   Centrality of Religion

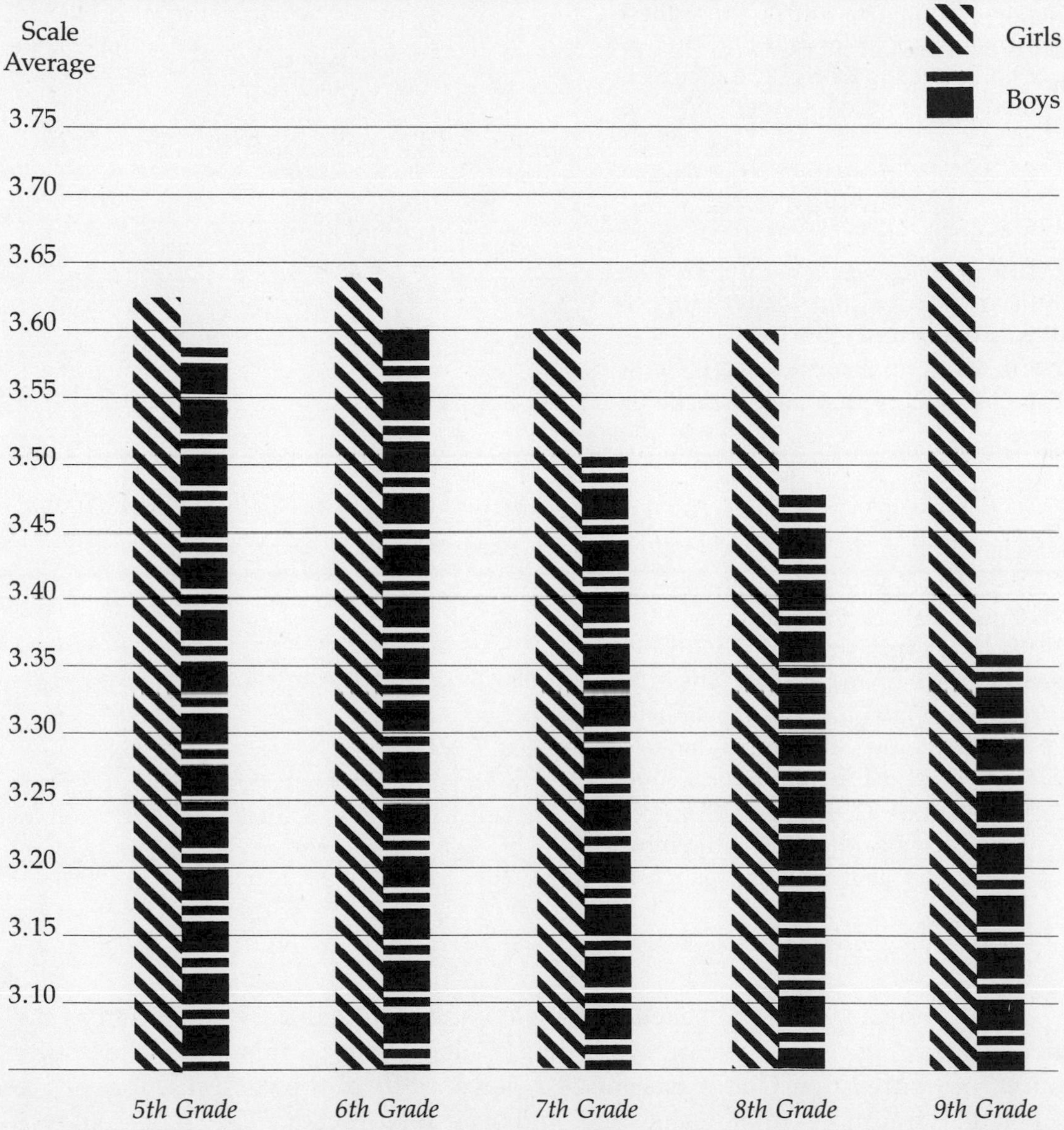

Scale
Average

| | Girls |
| Boys |

3.75
3.70
3.65
3.60
3.55
3.50
3.45
3.40
3.35
3.30
3.25
3.20
3.15
3.10

5th Grade   *6th Grade*   *7th Grade*   *8th Grade*   *9th Grade*

	5th	6th	7th	8th	9th	Total
Percent who agree with each of these statements about Jesus:						
I believe Jesus Christ is the Son of God who died on a cross and rose again.	85	88	88	89	87	87
I believe Jesus is the Son of God, but I doubt he actually rose from the dead.	7	6	5	5	5	6
I think Jesus was a great man who lived long ago, but I don't think he was the Son of God.	4	5	5	4	5	4
I don't think Jesus ever existed—it is just a story that people made up.	4	2	2	2	3	2

	5th	6th	7th	8th	9th	Total
Percent who agree with each of these statements about the Bible:						
I believe every word of the Bible is exactly what God wanted put in it.	58	54	49	47	47	51
I believe God guided the people who wrote the Bible, but I don't think every word came from God.	33	39	44	47	44	42
I don't think God had much to do with what's in the Bible—the Bible is just a lot of stories that people made up.	6	5	4	3	7	5
I don't know what the Bible is.	3	2	2	2	2	2

The young adolescents' beliefs about God and Jesus are very stable across the five grades. Eighty-six percent of all young adolescents in this study are "quite sure" or "sure" that God exists, and 87 percent affirm the central axiom of the Christian tradition—that Jesus died and was resurrected. These percentages parallel those reported in Gallup polls on the American adult population. In those polls, 94 percent of adults claim that God exists, and 83 percent affirm the divinity of Jesus.[7]

However, beliefs about the Bible do not show the same stability. From fifth to ninth grade, a shift away from the inerrant view (that God essentially dictated the Scriptures, word for word) occurs, and the percentage who take the position that God inspired the authors of the Bible, but did not "dictate," increases. It is significant that the shift occurs only between these two views. We found no evidence that young adolescents begin to perceive the Bible as human invention or that young adolescents become increasingly uncertain about "what the Bible is." At the ninth-grade level, 47 percent believe the Bible is inerrant. Gallup claims that 42 percent of American adults hold this position.[8] Denominations, of course, take varying positions on the inerrancy of Scripture. Those denominations that reject an inerrant view will applaud the trend away from belief in inerrancy; those that teach an inerrant view will be disappointed.

There may be evidence of cognitive or psychological development in this downturn on inerrancy. As their ability to think abstractly increases, young people begin to ponder the "reasonableness" of things and to try to discover for themselves what is true. This change in abilities generally presents a challenge to the belief, often accepted uncritically in childhood, that a divine, unseen force acts in the world. Faith meets reason, and conflict occurs. Perhaps the idea that God dictated the Bible seems too magical, so they abandon it as a childish thing to believe. A "reasonable" compromise for them may be to shift some of the Bible's origin to human beings, an occurrence that can be more easily observed and verified.[9] Had this study included older adolescents, we might have seen another shift, from an inspired view of Scripture to a "human invention" view, occurring among those for whom the conflict between faith and reason has become intense.

Adolescents experience a variety of consequences resulting from the "faith and reason" conflict that occurs during adolescence. Some permanently abandon the faith. Some temporarily enter a period of doubt and questioning out of which eventually springs a deeper conviction. And some never allow the conflict to impinge upon the faith. No researcher has yet explored these evolutions far enough to define how the church and family environments influence the paths youth take as they struggle with the claim of truth and authority.

As in the case of religious centrality, significant differences occur between the beliefs of boys and girls on each of the three statements about God, Jesus, and the Bible. Girls are more likely than boys to be certain about God's existence, to affirm the divinity of Jesus, and to accept an inerrant view of the Bible, and these differences are visible at each of the five grade levels (fifth through ninth).

RELIGIOUS THEMES

People experience religion in various ways. Individual people, even within the same religious denomination, differ in how they interpret and live out their faith. Those who know the inner workings of a congregation or parish know, for example, that some people want a congregation to emphasize evangelism, some want it to emphasize the teaching and preaching of the Word, and still others want it to emphasize social ministry. These various agendas spring, in part, from different belief emphases. We explored four of these emphases or themes in this study.

Liberating religion is the degree to which religion is experienced as freeing and enabling. People for whom religion is liberating place emphasis on the fact that God accepts them just as they are and that salvation is a gift, not something earned.

Restricting religion is the degree to which religion is experienced as supplying limits, control, guidelines, and discipline. Whereas liberating religion stresses freedom, restricting religion stresses limits.

Vertical religion (together with horizontal religion) has to do with how one interprets one's responsibility as a person of faith. Those with vertical orientation believe their priorities should be to establish and maintain a close relationship to God. The emphasis is on prayer, worship, and other activities that keep one's focus on God.

Horizontal religion is the religious force that impels people to reach out and care for other people. Themes of love and justice are central to a horizontal orientation.

These four themes come in different combinations. Some people demonstrate a strong emphasis on only one of the four dimensions—a horizontal orientation, for example, that becomes visible in the life of a person who is constantly reaching out, taking care of others. Some show strong emphasis on two of them—perhaps showing a sense of religion as restricting and a vertical orientation, which would lead to careful attention to rules and limits and a private kind of religion that does not frequently include actions demonstrating care for others. Some show little evidence of any of the four; some embrace all four about equally. We have demonstrated in *Religion on Capitol Hill: Myths and Realities* that knowing a person's position in relation to these four themes will help explain or even predict some of that person's actions.[10]

Figure 29 shows boys' and girls' relative positions on the liberating dimension. Students were asked to agree or disagree with each of three statements which were combined to show the degree to which young adolescents have a liberating orientation on a scale of 1 (low) to 5 (high).

My religious faith makes me feel as if a burden has been lifted from my shoulders.
I know God loves me just as I am.
I believe that if I do a lot of wrong things, God will stop loving me. (Scores for this statement were reversed.)

Figure 29   Liberating Religion

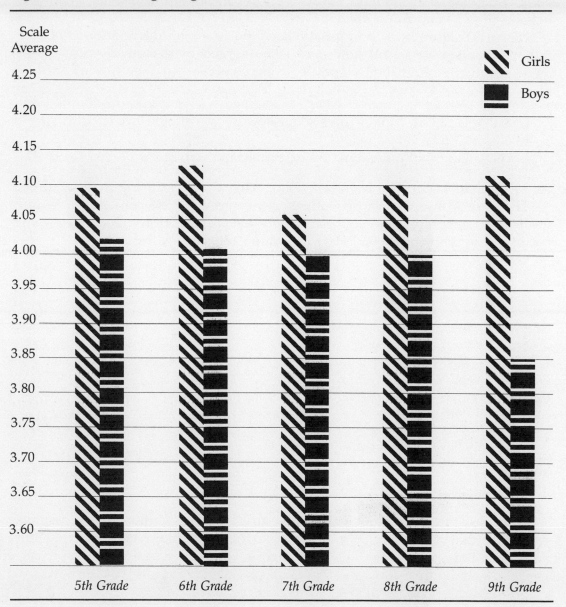

Overall, more young adolescents show evidence of a liberating orientation than of a restricting one. At each grade level, more girls experience religion as liberating than do boys,[11] and boys' sense of religion as liberating decreases markedly between eighth and ninth grade.

Figure 30 shows boys' and girls' relative positions on the restricting orientation. Students were asked how much they agreed or disagreed with each of three statements, and their responses were combined to show placement on a scale of 1 to 5.

I believe God has a lot of rules about how people should live their lives.
I believe God is very strict.
I believe God will punish me if I do something wrong.

At each grade level, more boys experience religion as restricting than do girls.

The vertical-horizontal orientations were measured by combining answers from four questions. One of these was: What do you think God most wants people to do with their lives? Here are young adolescents' responses:

	5th	6th	7th	8th	9th
God most wants people to pray. (Vertical)					
Percent of boys who agree	30	30	26	26	24
Percent of girls who agree	33	27	25	26	30
God most wants people to·work hard at getting rid of hunger and poverty. (Horizontal)					
Percent of boys who agree	18	16	20	19	20
Percent of girls who agree	12	14	16	15	13
God wants both of these in the same amount.					
Percent of boys who agree	52	54	54	55	56
Percent of girls who agree	55	58	59	59	57

Note that the percentage of boys and girls who choose the vertical response is similar; that more boys than girls choose the horizontal response while more girls than boys choose the "both" category, which is a balance of the vertical and horizontal dimensions; and that if a choice of either the vertical or horizontal response is made, more choose the vertical response.

When the four survey questions are combined (the one above plus three others like it), the following patterns emerge: (1) Boys tend to be slightly more horizontal in orientation than girls;[12] (2) The degree to which young adolescents adopt a horizontal orientation does not change significantly between fifth and

Figure 30   Restricting Religion

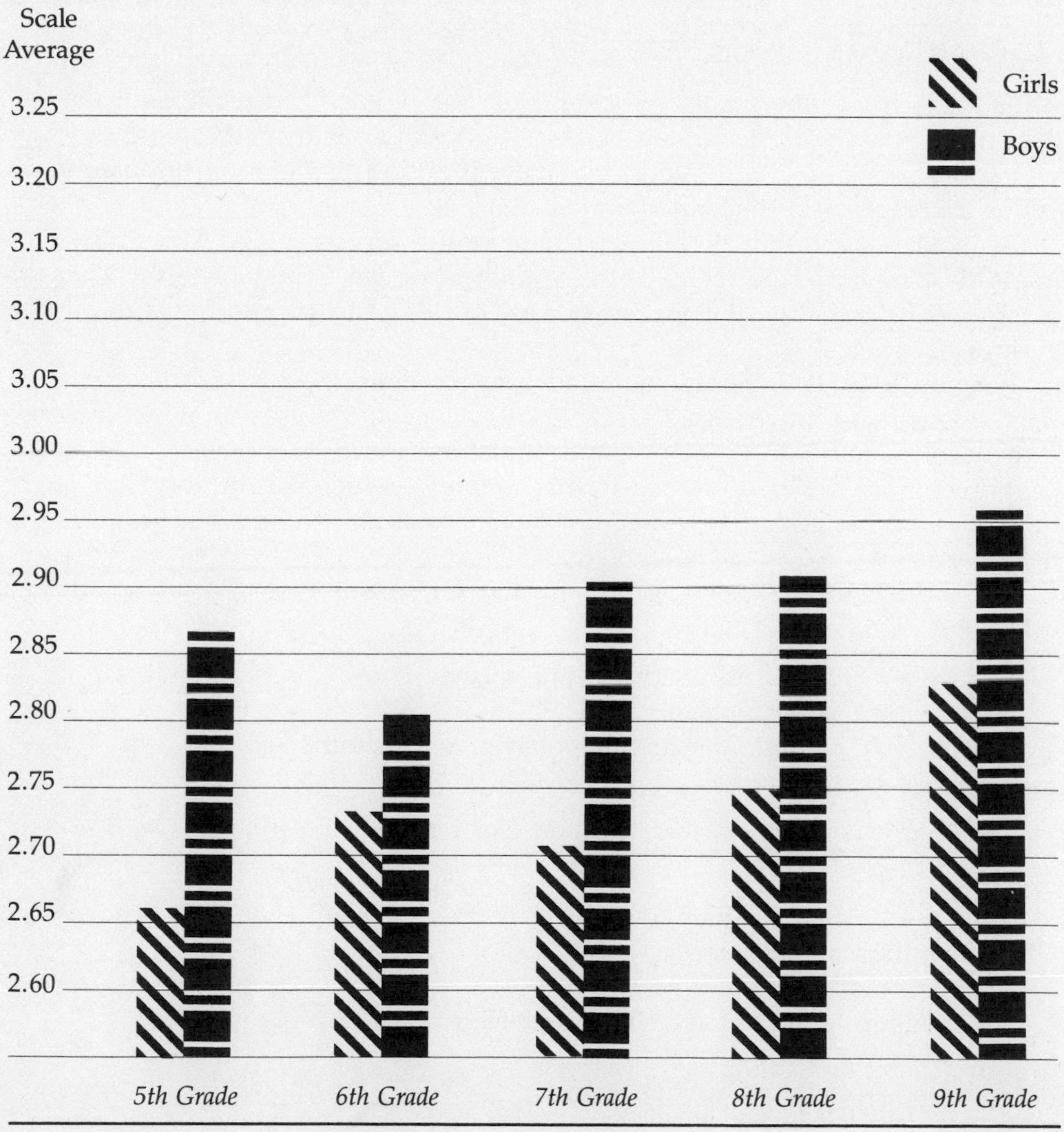

ninth grade; and (3) About 30 percent of young adolescents are vertically oriented, about 15 percent are horizontally oriented, and about 55 percent balance the vertical and horizontal dimensions.

SUMMARY AND CONCLUSIONS

This group of young adolescents mirrors the research on religious beliefs of the general public in the United States. This comparability indicates that what we report here apparently represents most if not all of the total population of young adolescents in the United States.

Religion is important to the majority of young adolescents in this study. The majority also subscribe to the orthodox tenets of the Christian faith. That is, most accept the reality of God, the divinity of Jesus Christ, and the authority of Scripture.

Religion tends to liberate young adolescents more than to restrict them. In part, this means that young adolescents hold a view of the creator of the universe as benevolent rather than judging and punishing.

Three of the scales discussed in this chapter—religious centrality, liberating religion, and horizontal religion—are tied to desirable values and patterns of behavior.

The more central religion is to them, the more likely it is that young adolescents will

—have a positive attitude toward the church
—have high self-esteem
—engage in helpful, considerate behavior toward others
—refrain from drug and alcohol use

The more they hold a liberating view of religion, the more likely it is that young adolescents will

—have a positive attitude toward the church
—have high self-esteem
—not be racially prejudiced
—engage in helpful, considerate behavior toward others
—refrain from drug and alcohol use
—refrain from antisocial behaviors

The more horizontal their orientation is, the more likely it is that young adolescents will

—place high value on world peace
—have a value orientation that emphasizes a concern for people[13]

The data in this chapter raise several issues of concern, particularly for those interested in the religious development of young adolescents. All of them, in one way or another, relate to the religious beliefs and perceptions of boys.

In general, religion is less important to boys than to girls. On the measure of centrality of religion, boys' scores are quite close to girls', but they begin a downward turn after sixth grade, a finding that reinforces the report in Chapter 2 that boys' commitment to the church also decreases after sixth grade. Further, the centrality of religion, for boys, takes another, sharper downturn after eighth grade, and this downturn is accompanied by a downturn in their perception of religion as liberating.

At the same time, boys' perceptions of religion as a restricting force rise. A strong sense of religion as a restricting force in one's life has several negative features. Young people who have high scores on restricting religion tend also to have high scores on antisocial behavior and alcohol use.[14] High restricting religion scores are also tied to racial prejudice and sexism.[15]

One possible explanation for these negative connections with a view of religion as restricting is that adolescents see religion presenting an expectation of high behavioral standards that may conflict with their desires to make their own decisions and chart their own course in life—the natural outcome of the near-universal desire to grow in autonomy and independence. The parent-child conflict that occurs when these two collide results in rebellion on the part of the young person, with alcohol use and other antisocial behaviors often being the vehicle of rebellion. An authoritarian parenting style, one that puts a hard edge between what is right and what is wrong, appears, from this and other research, also to breed prejudice.

Another explanation may be that when a young adolescent begins to exhibit problem behavior, the adults in the young person's life begin to use God "as a hammer," strengthening the young person's conviction that religion is principally composed of sets of rules and prohibitions. Evidence in the survey data shows that young adolescents who view religion as restricting tend also to experience coercive forms of discipline at home.[16]

Easy solutions to the problem this discovery presents do not spring immediately to mind. However, knowing that boys' reluctance to develop a too-close association with the church and with religion is a universal tendency and not simply a peculiarity of the religious institutions one knows best is likely to be useful. Boys' arms'-length posture toward the church also emphasizes the need to present religion to them in forms other than the restrictive, rule-setting mode.

CHAPTER 9

Prosocial Behavior

· **When asked how many hours they devoted to helping the sick, aged, poor, or handicapped, 34 percent of young adolescents reported giving no help; 40 percent said they had helped someone for one or two hours during the last month; and 26 percent reported having spent three hours or more giving such help.**

· **Based on a six-question index of prosocial behavior, girls report more prosocial behavior than boys at each grade between fifth and ninth.**

· **Young adolescents who help other people tend to come from families that are affectionate, nurturant, and democratic, and that practice inductive discipline.**

When adults in conversation talk about "kids these days," chances are that they are not talking about young people's goals, attitudes, or religious beliefs, but about their behavior.

Young people just entering the period of adolescence are not far from childhood, and, before that, infancy, in which most were objects of others' care and little was required of them in the way of help for others. Entry to adolescence marks for many the first time they discover that they can do things that are of practical help to others.

This survey provided young people with an opportunity to register their experience of helping others, and it also offered hypothetical situations in order to discover how many of them have attitudes that would incline them to offer help to others.

There are various types of prosocial behavior. Giving aid to a stranger who is injured or otherwise in trouble, sharing one's resources of money or food with those in need, giving volunteer time to charities, or assisting a friend or neighbor who needs help are all examples of prosocial behavior. The survey included two types of prosocial behavior: giving help that takes some time, such as raising money for the hungry or spending time with someone who is ill, elderly, or handicapped, and giving help on the spot, such as helping someone who has fallen down or helping a lost child find his or her parents.

Self-report of altruistic (prosocial) behaviors invites skepticism, no matter what the age group, and critics are especially likely to inquire about the "fudge factor" in the responses of this age group. Since prosocial behavior is obviously desirable, aren't young adolescents going to report what looks good rather than what is really true?

Several pieces of evidence suggest we *can* trust the self-reports of these young people. For one thing, we find a mathematical correlation between a young adolescent's report of prosocial behavior and his or her mother's rating of how much her child helps people. We also find that reports of prosocial behavior are consistent with the value young adolescents place on "doing things that help people."[1] These findings give us reason to believe the reports of young adolescent behavior we see in the survey responses.

One of the questions reads as follows:

Do you spend time giving help to people outside the family that have special needs (for example, collecting food for hungry people, or mowing lawns for people who can't do it themselves, or spending time with sick or handicapped people)? Think about the helpful things you have done in the last month—for which you did not get paid, but which you did because you wanted to be kind to someone else. About how many hours did you give help during the last month?

Their choice of answers and the percentages for all young adolescents combined are given here.

Hours of Help	*Percent of Young Adolescents*
None	34
1–2 hours	40
3–4 hours	16
5–10 hours	6
11 hours or more	4

Notably, about a third of the young people said they had done nothing, which may also support our assumption that, by and large, they are telling the truth on this question. Combined with the next category, we see that nearly three quarters of the young people say they spent two hours or less helping others.

The remaining 26 percent report helping others three hours or more during the last month.

Some questions probing prosocial behavior dealt with hypothetical situations in which the young adolescent was asked to report how he or she would respond to an emergency. In these cases, almost half report that they would help. However, as other research shows, some of those who report they would help in such situations do not do so when actually confronted with one. Two of these hypothetical situations are given below with the percentages of affirmative responses.

Imagine you saw a little kid fall and get hurt on a playground. Would you run over and try to help?
Percent of young adolescents who answered yes   51

Imagine yourself walking by a grocery store. You are alone and don't know any of the people around you. A woman drops a bag of groceries all over the sidewalk. Would you stop and help her pick up the groceries?
Percent of young adolescents who answered yes   42

When we combine the six prosocial questions into an overall index of prosocial behaviors (with 1 = low and 5 = high), the patterns shown in Figure 31 emerge. At each grade, girls report more prosocial inclination than boys. Girls' prosocial averages rise with grade, and boys' averages remain stable across grade level.[2] This pattern is consistent with the finding, outlined in Chapter 3, that girls tend more than boys to value and seek connections with people.

The following characteristics are associated with young adolescents who score high on prosocial behavior:

—a value orientation that shows concern for people
—achievement motivation
—acceptance of traditional moral values
—a nurturing family
—an affectionate family
—democratic control in the family
—inductive discipline by parents
—perception of school climate as positive
—positive attitudes toward the church
—centrality of religion
—liberating religion

Figure 31   Prosocial Behavior

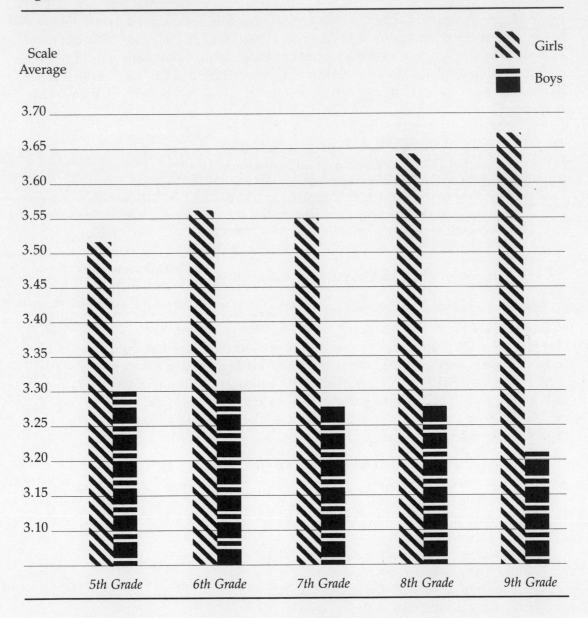

The following characteristics tend not to be associated with young adolescents who score high on prosocial behavior:

—racial prejudice
—sexism
—authoritarian control
—coercive discipline
—youth-parent conflict

Two characteristics in particular stand out. First, prosocial action is definitely related to positive feelings about school and several positive attitudes and behaviors related to church and religion. Second, certain parenting practices are closely tied to prosocial behavior of young adolescents. Children who have prosocial attitudes come from families in which affection is shown, both with tender talk and with hugs and kisses. They come from nurturing families in which parents pay careful attention to the child's needs and take time to listen to and talk with the child. They come from families that are democratically controlled, families in which the parent tries to set rules and guidelines cooperatively with the child and attempts to take the child's point of view into consideration when setting rules. They also come from families in which discipline is inductive—in which, when the child breaks a rule, the parent explains to the child why the rule is important, why the behavior was wrong, and how violations of rules conflict with the child's concern for others. Taken as a whole, this parenting style shows respect for the child and assures the child that he or she is affirmed and loved, even while the parent is in the process of helping the child learn how to live in an orderly world, respectful of others' rights and needs.[3]

CHAPTER 10

Antisocial Behavior

· Twenty-seven percent of young adolescents in this study report committing one or more acts of vandalism during the last twelve months.
· A *majority* of young adolescent boys (64 percent) and a significant minority of girls (32 percent) report they have "hit or beat up another kid during the last twelve months."
· Sixteen percent of boys report they have been involved in six or more fights during the last twelve months.
· In the fifth, sixth, and seventh grades, the majority report that they did not cheat on a test at school. In the eighth and ninth grades, more than 60 percent report cheating at least once in the last twelve months.
· About one out of five young adolescents in each of the five grades reports stealing something one or more times in the last twelve months.

Incessant activity is the hallmark of this age, probably as the result of energy released in the body to support the physical and mental growth of the young adolescent. And, perhaps because the development of judgment has not kept pace with the young person's potential to harm others, he or she frequently uses that fund of energy in ways adults disapprove of. Some of these behaviors are merely annoying, but adults classify some as antisocial and will do their best to prevent or to stop them, if they can.

We use the term *antisocial behavior* to refer to two kinds of action: physical aggression or violence, and standard breaking—violation of adult social standards by such actions as lying, cheating, and stealing. Much as adults hope that young adolescents will avoid these behaviors, we find them occurring with some frequency and becoming more frequent as the child progresses from fifth to ninth grade. The responses to the following question show the increase and the widespread nature of such behavior.

	5th	6th	7th	8th	9th
I do a lot of things I hope my parents never find out about.					
Percent who "agree" with the statement	26	28	34	40	42
Percent who are "not sure"	21	21	20	19	18
Percent who "disagree"	53	51	46	41	40

The percentage of young people who agree that there are actions they hope to conceal from their parents grows steadily through the grades, with major jumps between sixth and seventh grades, and again between seventh and eighth grade. At the same time, the percentage of those who are not sure and those who disagree steadily diminishes.

PHYSICAL AGGRESSION

The period of seventh, eighth, and ninth grades, the junior high school years, sees the peak of victimization among youth toward other youth. What makes this victimizing so heartbreaking to watch is that the victims, like the victimizers, are living through a period of great vulnerability, a period when the good opinion and the friendship of peers means so much to them. They are all engaged in a search for identity, achievement, and social competence. Some try to find it by subjecting others to their verbal or physical aggression. Name-calling, punching, shoving, racing to be first in line, teasing others by grabbing an item of clothing or a book, taunting, chanting, ignoring—all of these are part of the everyday life experience of young adolescents. For some, the victimizing or being victimized goes no further than this. But for some, the desperate drive to feel power over others leads to more serious activity such as vandalism, hitting to hurt, and group fighting. The survey asked a question related to each of these three actions. The questions and young adolescents' responses follow.

During the last twelve months, how often have you damaged or destroyed property (for example, broken windows or furniture, put paint on walls or signs, put scratches or dents in a car) at school or somewhere else?

	Percent of Young Adolescents				
Number of Times	*5th*	*6th*	*7th*	*8th*	*9th*
None	78	76	73	70	69
Once or twice	12	14	16	18	18
3–5 times	4	4	6	6	6
6–10 times	3	3	3	3	4
11 times or more	3	3	2	2	3
Once or more	22	24	27	30	31

During the last twelve months, how often have you hit or beat up another kid?

	5th	*6th*	*7th*	*8th*	*9th*
None	55	53	50	52	56
Once or twice	24	25	24	28	24
3–5 times	10	11	13	10	9
6–10 times	5	5	7	5	5
11 times or more	5	6	6	6	6
Once or more	45	47	50	48	44

During the last twelve months, how often have you taken part in a fight where a group of friends fought another group?

	5th	*6th*	*7th*	*8th*	*9th*
None	70	70	74	74	79
Once or twice	17	18	15	15	11
3–5 times	8	6	6	5	5
6–10 times	2	3	2	3	2
11 times or more	3	3	2	3	3
Once or more	30	30	26	26	21

In all cases, the majority say they have not been involved in these aggressive behaviors. Nonetheless, a significant percentage report that they have. Three findings stand out:

· Nearly half report hitting or beating up another person.
· About one out of every four reports one or more acts of vandalism.
· About one out of every four reports involvement in one or more group fights.

Although most of these incidents are probably not the kinds of gang wars often depicted in the media, this form of aggression needs to be taken seriously, since groups frequently carry a conflict to more serious acts than individuals would undertake if acting alone.

On the positive side, the percentage of young adolescents who engage in aggressive acts more than once or twice is relatively small, with only 11 percent reporting hitting or beating up more than once or twice, and 6 percent or less reporting vandalism or group fighting more than once or twice.

Figures 32, 33, and 34 show substantial boy-girl differences in aggression. In all three cases, boys report considerably more. Note, however, that substantial numbers of girls are involved in acts of aggression "once or more." Combining the grades, we see that 18 percent of girls report engaging in vandalism, 32 percent "hitting or beating up," and 21 percent "group fighting." Boys' aggression increases with grade and peaks at the eighth grade, while girls' aggression declines slightly from fifth to ninth grade.[1]

STANDARD-BREAKING BEHAVIORS

The survey contained questions about shoplifting, cheating, and lying. The questions and young adolescents' responses follow.

Figure 32   Vandalism

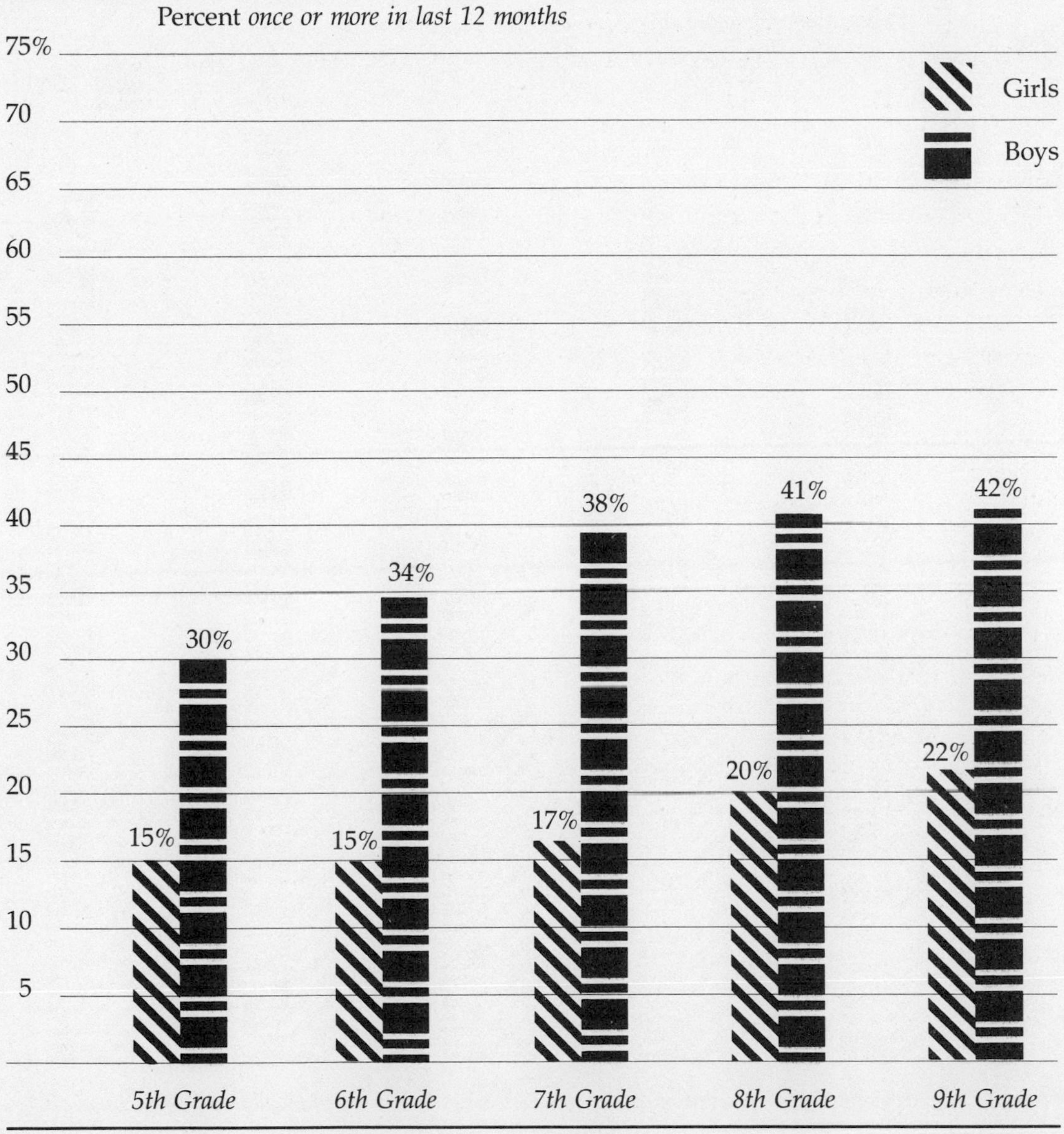

Percent *once or more in last 12 months*

Figure 33   Frequency of "Hitting or Beating Up Another Kid"

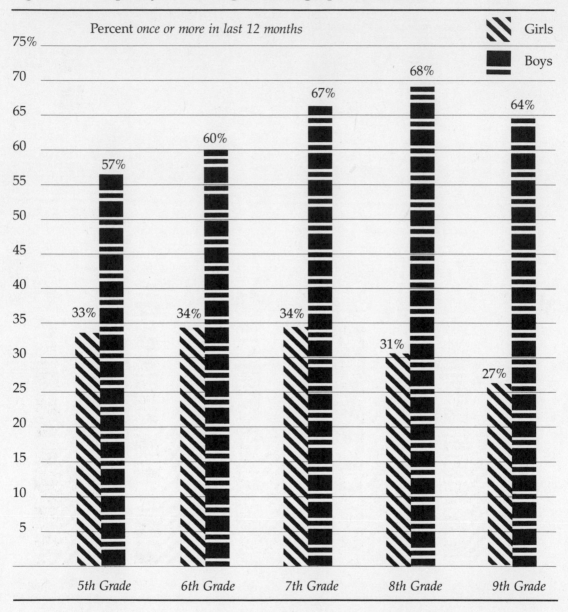

Figure 34   Gang Fighting

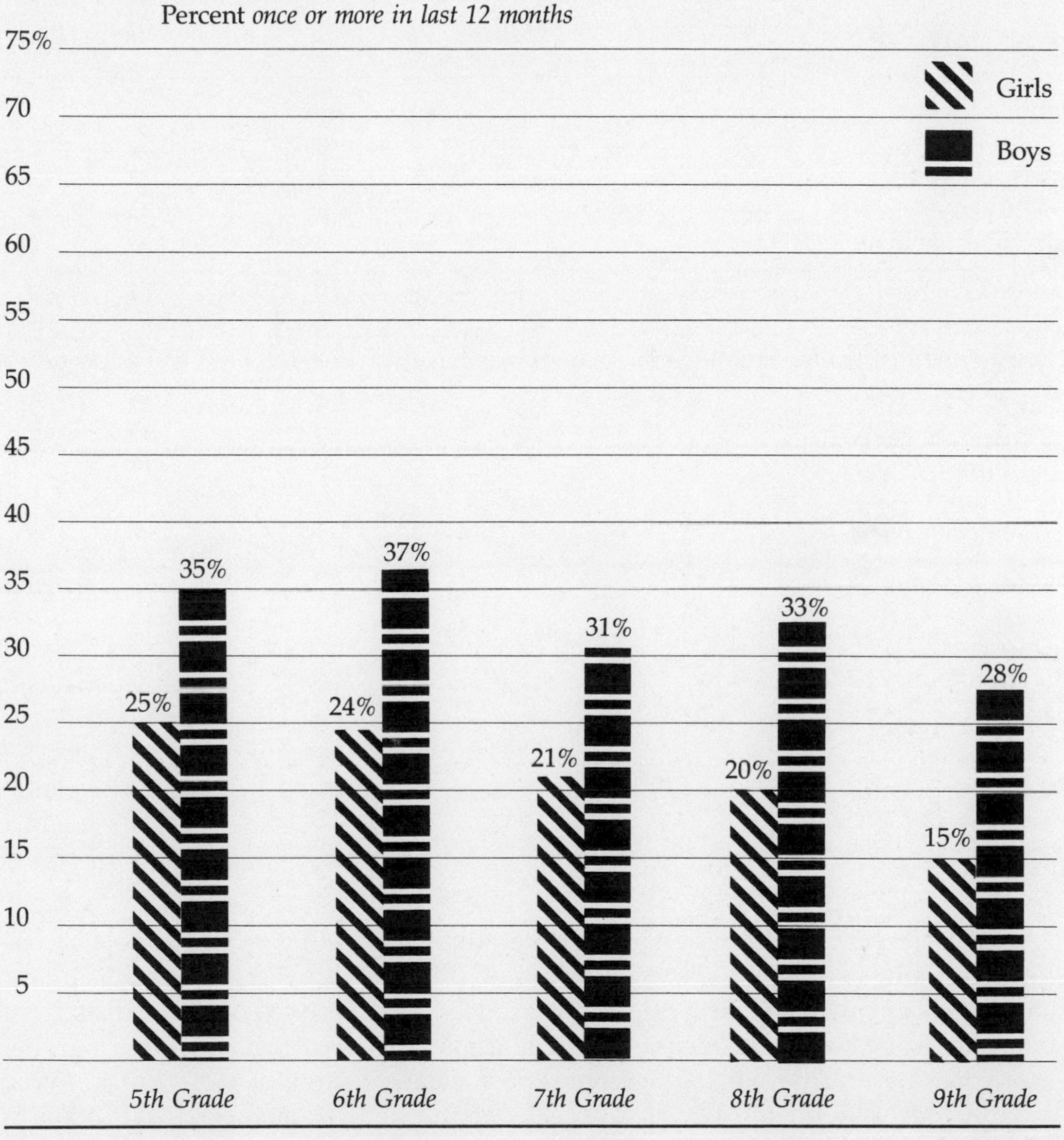

Percent *once or more in last 12 months*

75%

70

65

60

55

50

45

40

35%   37%

35

31%   33%

30   28%

25%   24%

25   21%   20%

15%

20

15

10

5

Girls
Boys

5th Grade   6th Grade   7th Grade   8th Grade   9th Grade

During the last twelve months, how often have you taken something from a store without paying for it?

			Percent of Young Adolescents			
Number of Times	*5th*	*6th*	*7th*	*8th*	*9th*	*Total*
None	81	82	81	81	81	81
Once or twice	9	9	9	10	9	9
3–5 times	4	5	4	5	5	5
6–10 times	4	3	3	2	3	3
11 times or more	2	2	3	2	3	2
Once or more	19	18	19	19	19	19

During the last twelve months, how many times have you cheated on a test at school?

None	67	60	53	39	33	50
Once or twice	20	26	30	35	37	30
3–5 times	6	7	9	14	17	11
6–10 times	4	3	4	7	7	5
11 times or more	3	3	4	5	7	4
Once or more	33	40	47	61	67	50

During the last twelve months, how often have you lied to one of your parents?

None	26	22	18	14	12	18
Once or twice	38	41	39	38	34	38
3–5 times	18	17	20	21	23	20
6–10 times	7	9	11	11	13	10
11 times or more	11	11	12	15	17	13
Once or more	74	78	82	86	88	82

The percentages of boys and girls who admit to stealing remain stable across the five grades. On the other two forms of standard breaking, however, major changes occur between fifth and ninth grade. Cheating once or more rises from one third of young adolescents at fifth grade to two thirds by ninth grade. Moreover, by ninth grade, 30 percent report cheating three or more times. Lying also increases, with the largest increases at the high frequency levels of six to ten times and eleven times or more.

As in the case of physical aggression, the percentages are much higher for boys than for girls. They are also higher on stealing and cheating. (See Figures 35 and 36.) On frequency of lying, boys and girls are quite similar. Standard

Figure 35   Stealing

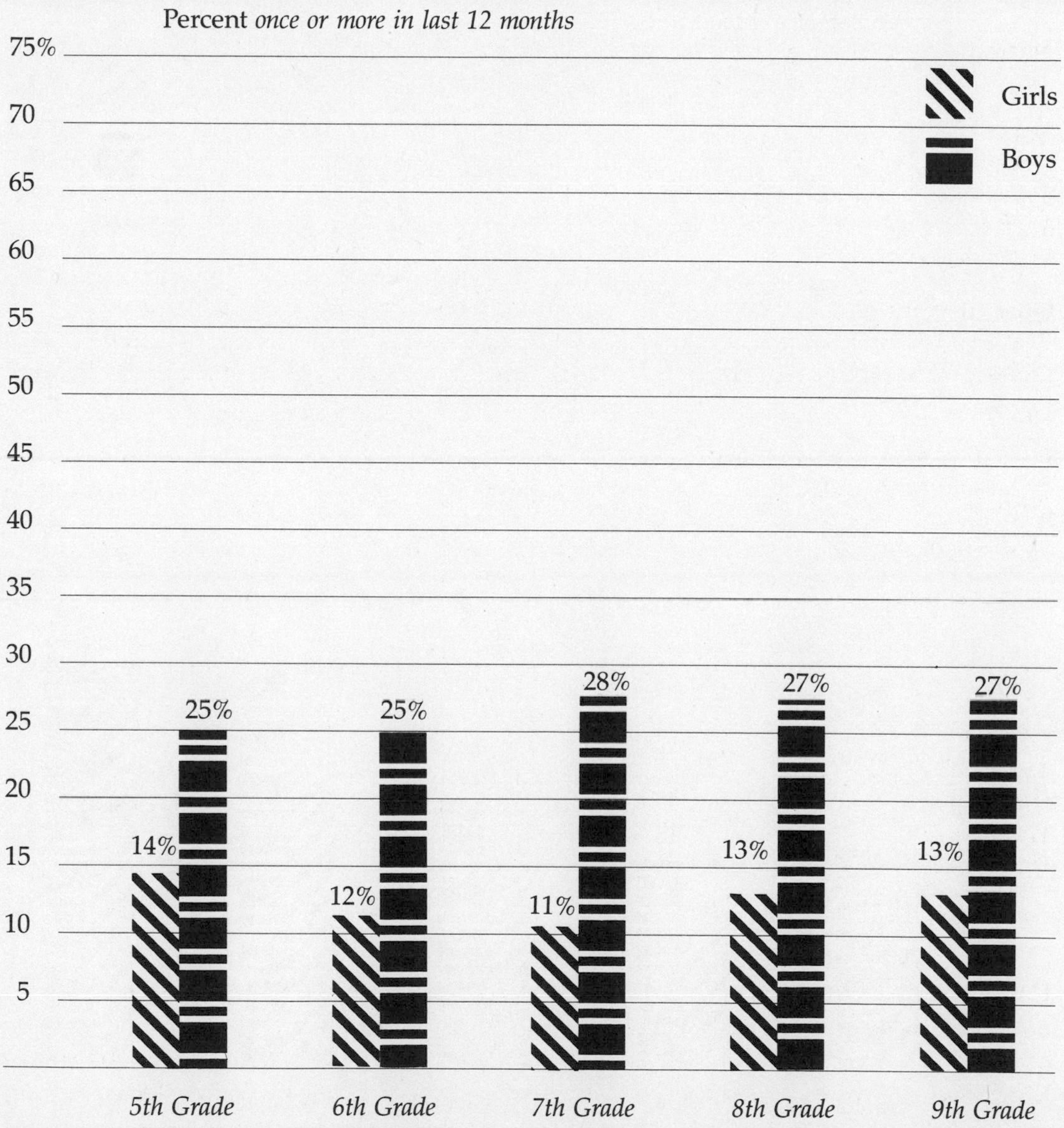

Percent *once or more in last 12 months*

75%

70

65

60

55

50

45

40

35

30

25%   25%   28%   27%   27%

25

20

15   14%   12%   11%   13%   13%

10

5

5th Grade   6th Grade   7th Grade   8th Grade   9th Grade

Girls

Boys

Figure 36   Cheating

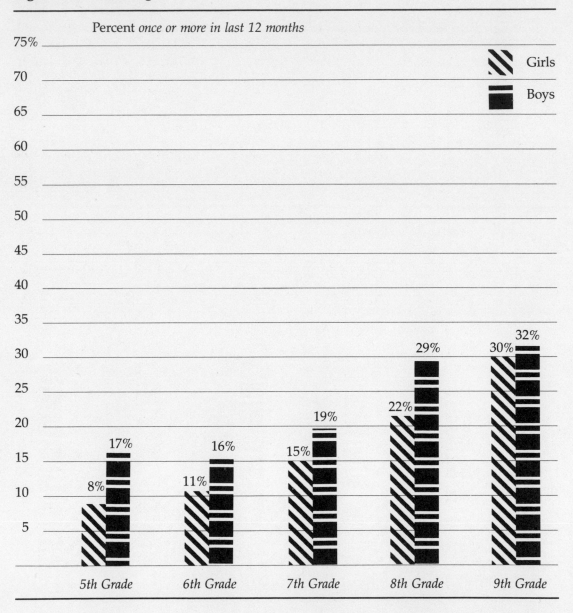

Percent *once or more in last 12 months*

breaking is high for boys at each grade level, with boys and girls reporting a similar increase between fifth and ninth grade.[2]

The findings reported in this chapter are consistent with those cited in other research. Most studies show the kind of sex differences reported here, and most show an increase through the junior high years in standard-breaking behavior.[3]

While it may be a small comfort to know these patterns are found in other studies, two findings are particularly disquieting:

One in four young adolescents reports vandalism.
Cheating once or more becomes the norm by eighth grade.

Both aggression and standard breaking are more likely to occur when a young adolescent

—associates with peers who are prone to this kind of deviance
—experiences conflict with parents
—is not interested in school
—has a great deal of exposure to the media
—perceives school climate as negative (that is, peers at school abuse chemicals, break rules, and do not take school seriously).[4]

Parents' age-old concerns that their child may be influenced by "running with a bad crowd" are justified in these findings.

CHAPTER 11

Chemical Use

· Boys report considerably more use of alcohol and marijuana than do girls.
· Experimentation with alcohol is more common among current fifth graders than it was among older youth when they were in the fifth grade.
· The percentage of youth who drank alcohol ten or more times "in the last twelve months" doubles between the eighth and ninth grades.
· During the twelve months prior to the survey
  More than one in five (22%) fifth graders report alcohol use.
  Among ninth graders, more than half (53%) have used alcohol.
  Forty-seven percent of ninth graders attended a party at which peers were drinking.
  Thirteen percent of all young adolescents in this study report using marijuana.

One of our recurring themes is that today's young adolescents face issues and decisions that used to be reserved for older youth. Generally speaking, young adolescents today are less sheltered from the adult world than were previous generations of ten- to fourteen-year-olds. In Chapter 3, we discussed young adolescents' involvement in the complex arena of sexuality. In Chapter 4, we noted that fifth and sixth graders express concern about violence and global affairs. And in this chapter, we will see that many young adolescents are making decisions about alcohol and drugs.

One observer of this acceleration into the adult world suggests that "children today *know more, are freer,* and *grow up more rapidly*." These interrelated trends reinforce each other. Increased knowledge begets freedom, and freedom allows for the acquisition of knowledge. More autonomous and armed with greater knowledge, children emerge from childhood more rapidly.[1] The advent of television may be one of the factors causing this acceleration. "By virtue of television, the child enters the world of adults almost from the very beginning of life (or from the time the child has access to adult programs and can begin to understand them), hears the same language, much of the same level of discourse, and receives the same information. Some of the mystery and the difference between the life of the child and the adult no longer exists. In this sense, the child and the adult are peers and are thrust into the same stream of life from the very beginning; the child no longer trails in the footsteps of the parent with gaze fixed on the leader."[2] Whether or not this is true is one question; and if true, whether or not it's good is another. Certainly in the case of substance abuse this early knowledge and entry into the adult world has had some tragic results.

The survey contained a series of questions about chemical use, covering the areas of alcohol, marijuana, cigarettes, and "other drugs." Here, again, skeptics may raise their eyebrows. Will youth tell the truth when they are asked to report on something personal, and perhaps self-incriminating, like drug use? We believe that, for the most part, they do. Respondents to this survey were assured of confidentiality and were not asked for personal identifiers such as their name. Evidence based on other studies suggests that students protected in this way give true reports of their chemical use. For example, researchers have consistently found that survey data from a local community or geographical region corresponds to data gathered by other methods of inferring drug-use patterns, such as "urinalysis for drug use, polygraph verification, official police, court, and treatment agency documents, and reports by peers, parents, and teachers."[3] Other research has also found that intentional overreporting of drug use is minimal.

ALCOHOL

How often, if at all, do young adolescents drink alcohol? We asked them a similar question in the survey, and their responses are given here.

In the last twelve months, have you had beer, wine, or liquor to drink? (Do not count the times you took a sip of someone else's drink.)

| Number of Times | Percent of Young Adolescents | | | | |
	5th	6th	7th	8th	9th
None	78	75	69	58	47
1 or 2 times	10	12	16	20	20
3–9 times	8	9	10	15	19
10 times or more	4	4	5	7	14
Once or more	22	25	31	42	53

Three findings stand out:

· More than one in five (22 percent) fifth graders report alcohol use in the last year.
· By ninth grade, more than half (53 percent) have used alcohol in the last year.
· The percentage of youth who drank alcohol ten or more times in the last year doubles between the eighth and ninth grade.

A second survey item explored the issue of "getting drunk." It is not clear to what extent the younger of these young adolescents know what this term means, so the findings should be treated cautiously.

In the last twelve months, have you had so much alcohol to drink that you got drunk?

| | Percent of Young Adolescents | | | | |
Number of Times	5th	6th	7th	8th	9th
None	88	89	87	83	72
1 or 2 times	4	4	5	8	11
3–9 times	6	4	5	6	8
10 times or more	3	3	3	3	8
Once or more	12	11	13	17	28

A third question was worded as follows:

If you have ever drunk beer, wine, or liquor, how old were you when you had your first drink? (Don't count taking a sip of someone else's drink).

| | Percent of Young Adolescents | | | | |
Number of Times	5th	6th	7th	8th	9th
Percent who say they were ten years old or younger when they first used alcohol	27	23	19	15	15

The responses to this question give us an important piece of information. Almost twice as many fifth graders reported experimentation with alcohol by age ten as did eighth and ninth graders. If this report is to be trusted, use of alcohol by the age of ten is on the increase. Figures 37 and 38 show sizable sex differences in alcohol use, with boys reporting more use at each of the five grades.

One setting in which drinking occurs is parties, particularly for eighth and ninth graders, as the following figures show.

In the last year, how often have you been at a party where kids your age were drinking beer or liquor?

| | Percent of Young Adolescents | | | | |
Number of Times	5th	6th	7th	8th	9th
Not at all	89	88	82	70	53
Once or twice	6	8	11	18	21
Three times or more	5	4	7	12	26
Once or more	11	12	18	30	47

Note the significant increase between eighth and ninth grade of young people who have attended such parties three or more times. At every age level, boys are from 3 percent to 8 percent more likely than girls to attend parties at which drinking occurs.

MARIJUANA

Our survey also explored use of marijuana by young adolescents. Their responses follow:

In the last twelve months, have you used marijuana (pot, grass, dope)?

| | Percent of Young Adolescents | | | | |
Number of Times	5th	6th	7th	8th	9th
None	88	90	90	88	79
1 or 2 times	3	3	3	4	6
3–9 times	5	4	5	5	7
10 times or more	3	3	3	4	7
Once or more	12	10	10	13	20

One out of five ninth graders reports use during the last twelve months, with

Figure 37   Alcohol Use, Last Twelve Months

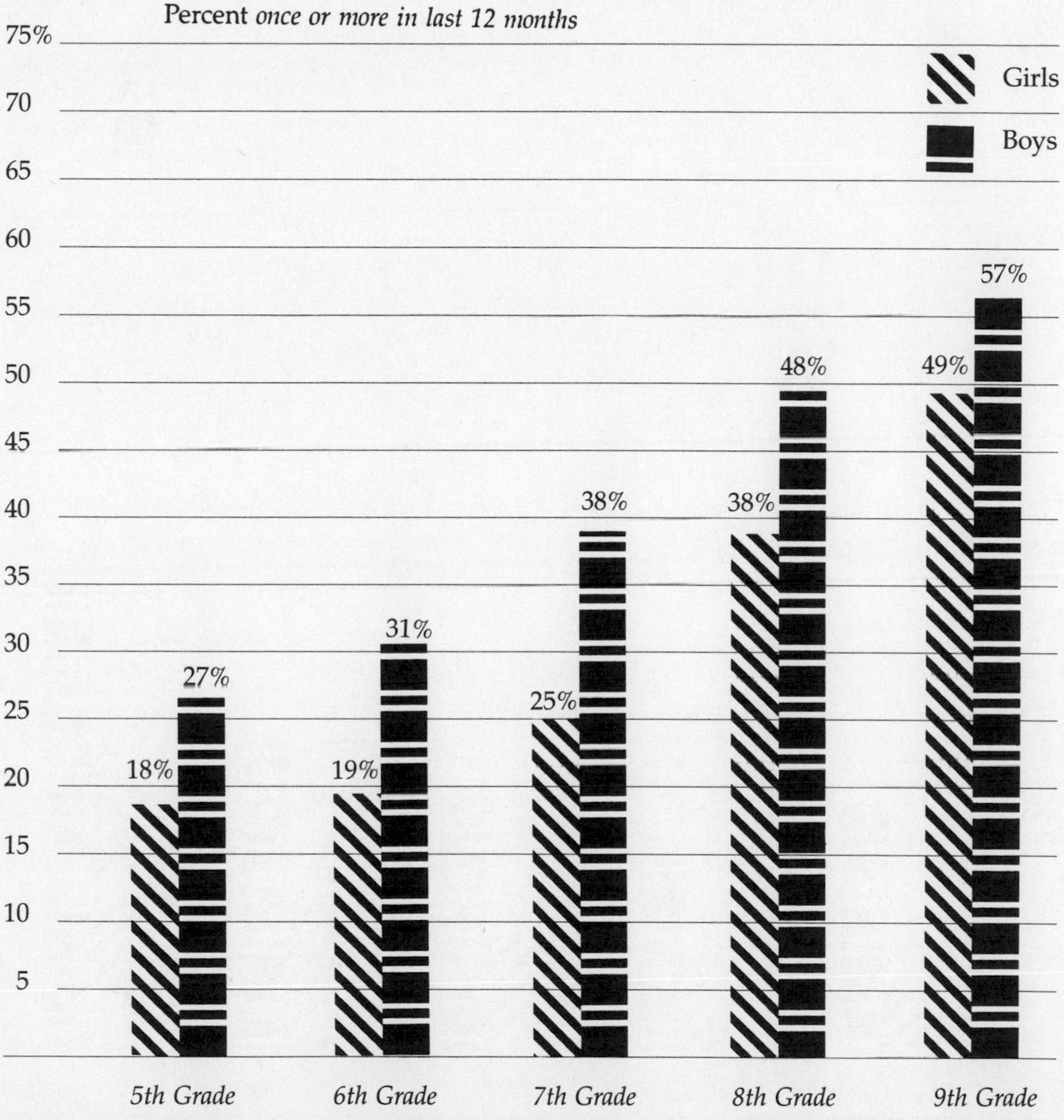

Figure 38 Percent Who Report Being Drunk, Last Twelve Months

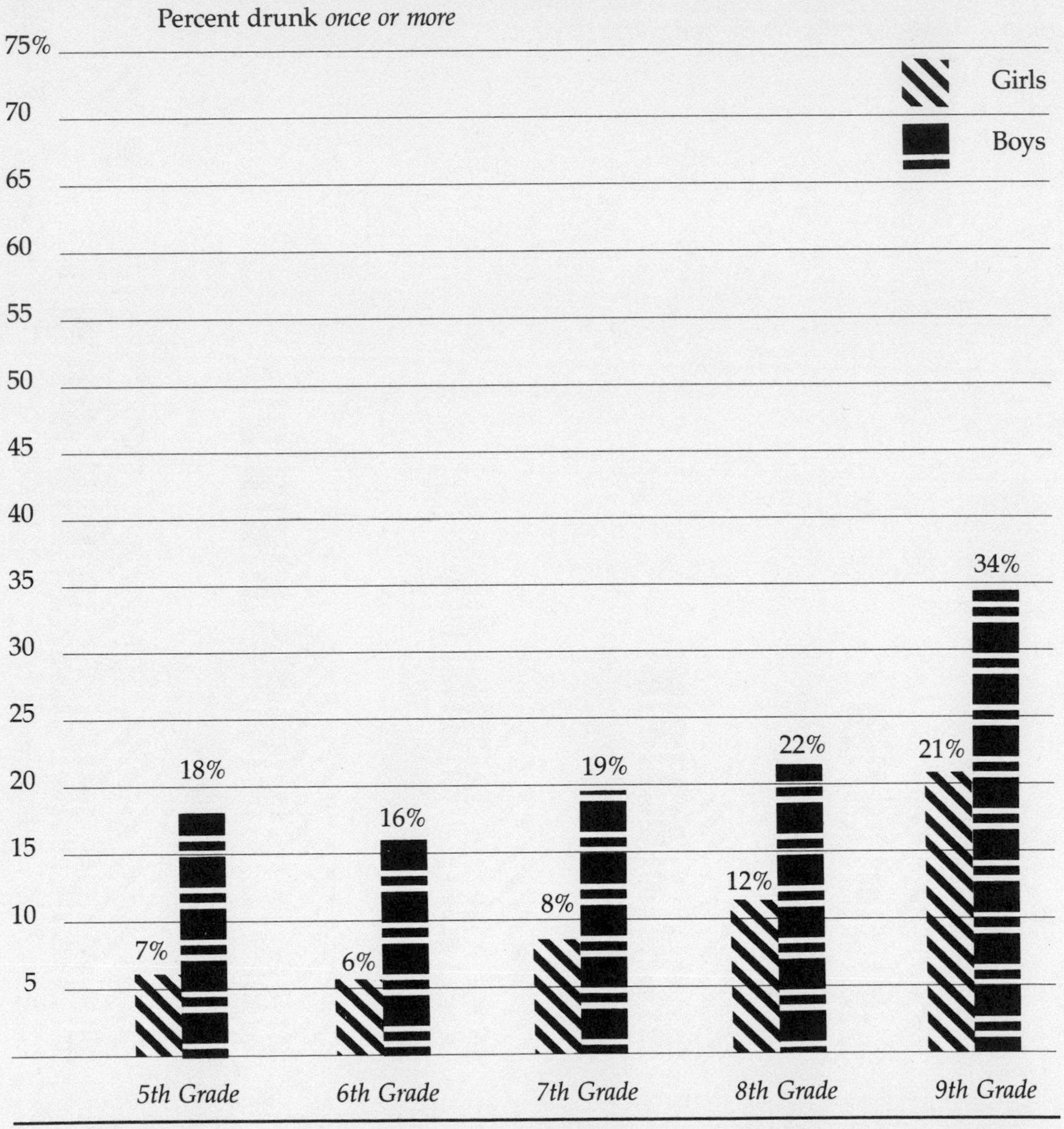

Percent drunk *once or more*

14 percent reporting use three or more times. Boys are more than twice as likely as girls to report use once or more. (See Figure 39.)

We noted that use of alcohol by age ten was much higher for fifth graders than ninth graders. This pattern does not hold for marijuana use, however, as shown below.

If you have ever tried marijuana (pot, grass, dope), how old were you when you first tried it?

	5th	6th	7th	8th	9th
Percent who say they were ten years old or younger when they first used marijuana	4	3	3	3	4

CIGARETTES

One survey question asked about cigarette smoking. The responses are listed below.

In the last twelve months, have you smoked a cigarette?

	Percent of Young Adolescents				
Number of Times	5th	6th	7th	8th	9th
No	81	79	77	70	64
1 or 2 times	6	9	9	13	12
3–9 times	7	7	8	9	9
10 or more times	6	5	6	8	15
Once or more	19	21	23	30	36

The rate of cigarette use (once or more) nearly doubles between the fifth and ninth grades. Note that the percentages for cigarette use are lower than for alcohol at each of the five grades. As in the cases of alcohol and marijuana, boys use cigarettes more than girls. (See Figure 40.)

OTHER DRUGS

Two survey items asked for information about use of other substances. One covered what are commonly called hard drugs, and the other, pill usage. This

Figure 39   Marijuana Use, Last Twelve Months

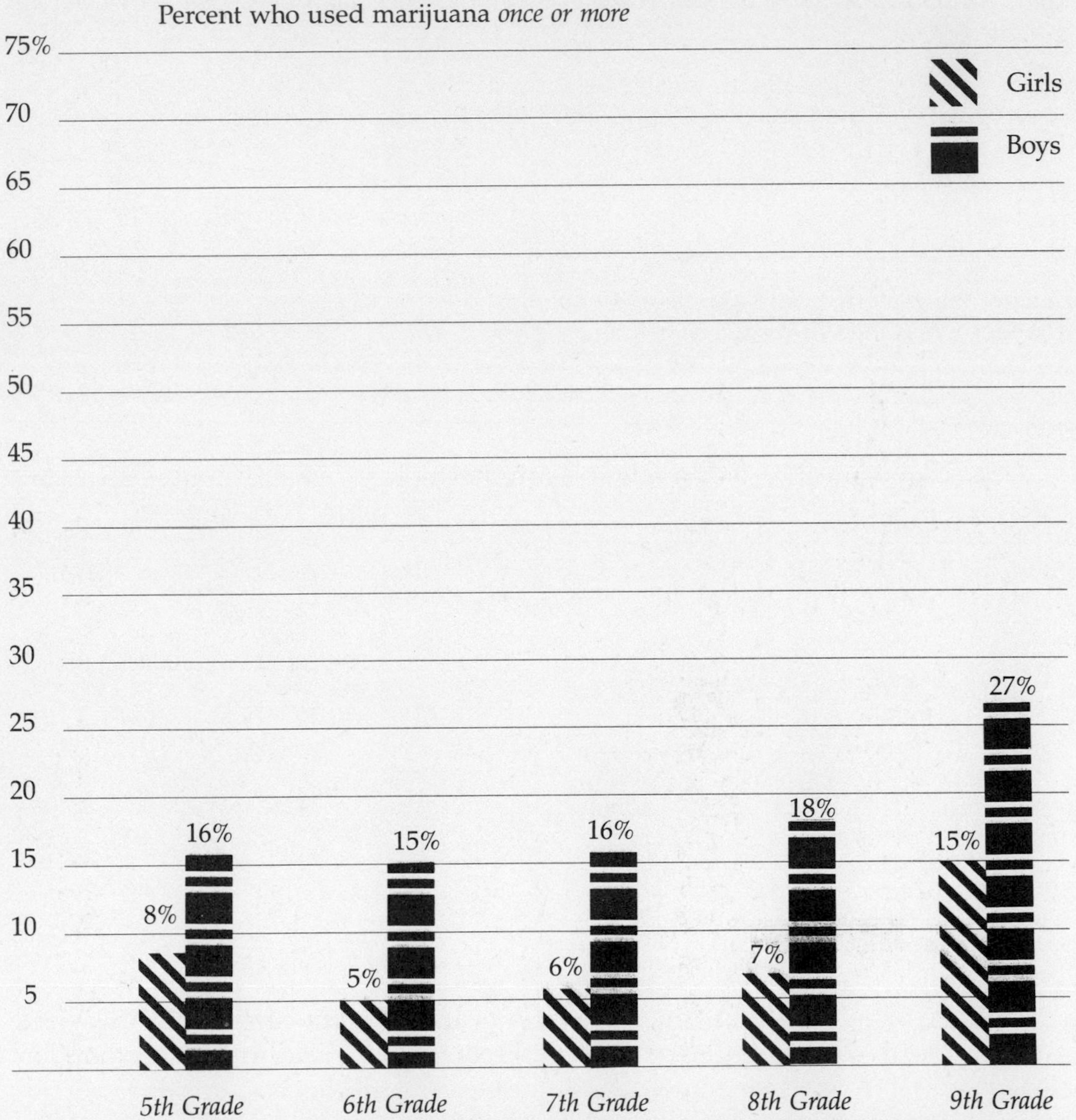

Percent who used marijuana *once or more*

Girls

Boys

5th Grade — 8%, 16%
6th Grade — 5%, 15%
7th Grade — 6%, 16%
8th Grade — 7%, 18%
9th Grade — 15%, 27%

Figure 40   Cigarette Smoking, Last Twelve Months

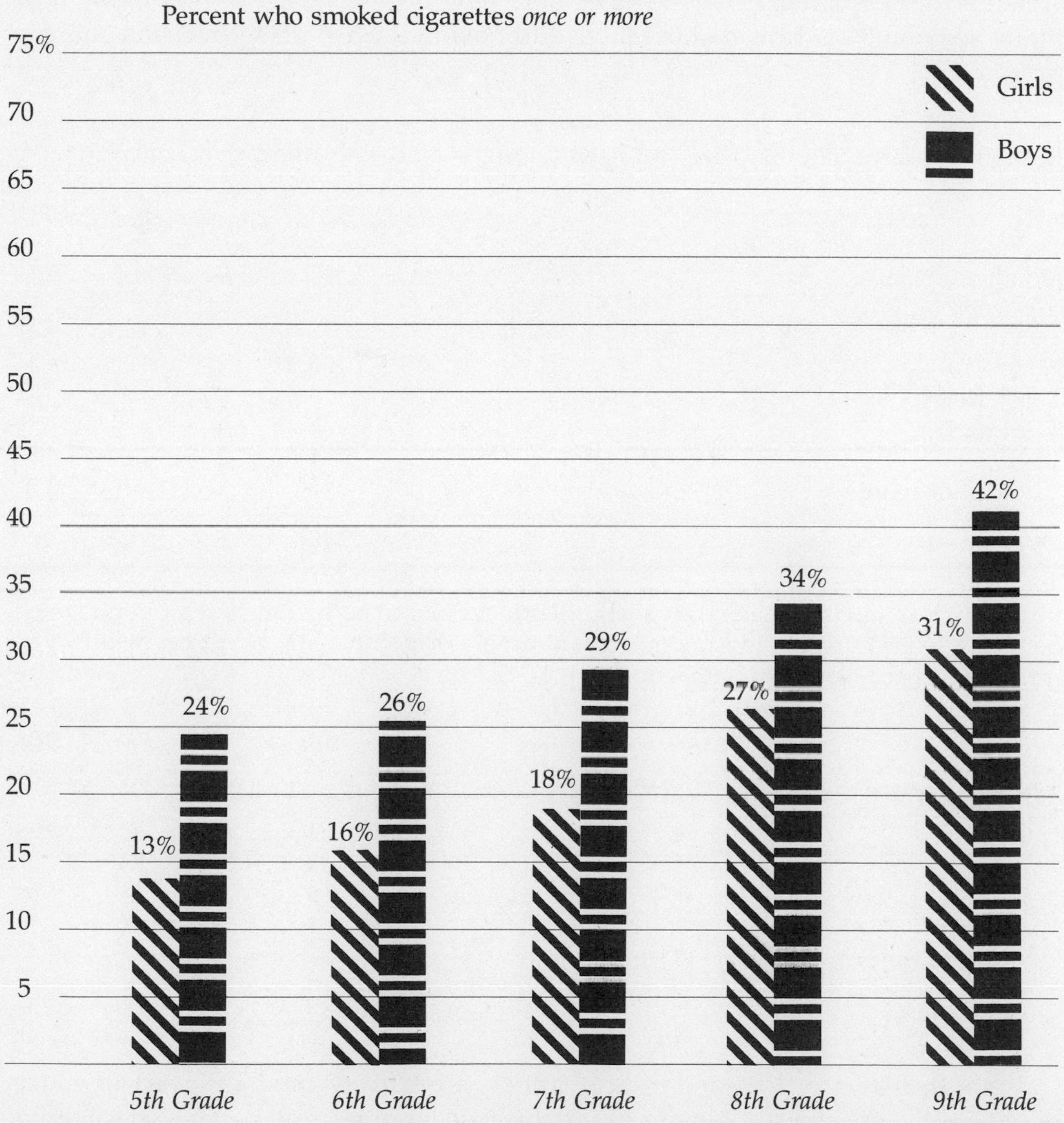

Percent who smoked cigarettes *once or more*

second item is a catch-all for a number of substances including *controlled substances*, like amphetamines, quaaludes, barbiturates, and *over-the-counter pills* or ''look-alike'' (products that look like amphetamines but contain uncontrolled substances like caffeine). We cannot sort out, on the basis of this item, how many are using controlled substances and how many are using over-the-counter products.

In the last twelve months, have you used a drug like cocaine, angel dust, or LSD?

| | Percent of Young Adolescents | | | | |
Number of Times	5th	6th	7th	8th	9th
None	88	90	92	92	90
1 or 2 times	3	3	2	3	3
3–9 times	6	5	4	4	3
10–19	1	1	1	1	1
20 times or more	1	2	1	1	2
Once or more	12	10	8	8	10

In the past 12 months, have you taken pills to get more energy (such as uppers, speed, bennies, dexies) or pills to relax (such as downers or goofballs)? (Don't count pills you have taken because of a doctor's orders.)

	5th	6th	7th	8th	9th
None	86	91	91	90	85
1 or 2 times	4	3	3	3	5
3–9 times	7	4	5	4	5
10–19 times	1	1	1	1	1
20 or more times	2	1	1	2	4
Once or more	14	9	9	10	15

In both the hard drug and pill categories, a relatively small minority of young adolescents report use. Almost all of this use seems to be of an experimental nature. Only one percent report high-frequency (use twenty times or more) of a hard drug substance, and only 2 percent report high-frequency use of pills, which suggests that young adolescents' problems with habitual use, or chemical dependency, are relatively rare in these categories.

SUMMARY

Information in this chapter leads us to three overall conclusions.

· Alcohol is clearly the substance with which young adolescents have the most experience, with 35 percent of all young adolescents in the survey reporting use once or more during the twelve months prior to the survey and more than half of ninth graders reporting some use.
· Although use of chemical substances for most of this group appears to be experimental and infrequent (use three times or less in the last year), a significant percentage of ninth graders report more frequent use. Fourteen percent report drinking alcohol ten times or more in the twelve months prior to the survey and 7 percent report marijuana use ten times or more.
· There is evidence that experimentation with alcohol is more common among current fifth graders than it was for eighth and ninth graders when they were in the fifth grade.

Not much is known about how young adolescents learn about drugs and alcohol and what factors help them make responsible choices about chemical use. What we do know from this survey is that one third of young adolescents want to talk more with their parents about drugs and alcohol and 65 percent express interest in having access to new school, club, or church programs dealing with drugs and alcohol (see Chapter 16).

Some readers might infer that drug and alcohol use in this sample of primarily "churched" youth would be much lower than it is for young adolescents in general. The available evidence, however, suggests otherwise. The use rates found in a recent national study of alcohol and marijuana use sponsored by the National Institute on Drug Abuse[4] are quite comparable to these.

Because they are aware of the tendency for adolescents to be peer-oriented and to try to fit into the contemporary youth culture, some adults have made the assumption that drug and alcohol use by adolescents is beyond the control of social institutions like family and church. We are less pessimistic. Strong mathematical relationships exist between chemical use and several family and religious variables. Because the relationships are correlational, we cannot be sure what causes what; we can only assert that there is a connection between them. The correlations suggest that certain family and religion variables may have an impact on young adolescents' involvement with drugs and alcohol.[5]

For example, we know that young adolescents are *less* likely to use alcohol and drugs when the following factors measured in this study are present to a high degree:

Family nurturance
Sense of closeness in the family
Family affection
Commitment of the young person to the church
Centrality of religion[6]

We know that young adolescents are *more* likely to use alcohol and drugs when the following are high:

Coercive discipline in the family
Authoritarian control in the family

A 1983 survey of ten thousand high school students in the state of Minnesota made an important discovery about the connection between family and church on the one hand and teenage drug use on the other. The single most powerful factor in non-use of alcohol and other drugs among this group was the degree to which the young person believed her or his parents would be upset to discover that they had been drinking. Three other variables—degree of activity in church youth groups, frequency of attendance at worship, and the importance to the young person of religion—showed the next most powerful connections with non-use of drugs.[7]

Part 2

YOUNG ADOLESCENTS AND THEIR FAMILIES

CHAPTER 12

How Parents View Their Children's World

· **Parents believe that the most positive influence on their children's lives are their own home, their teachers, and the church or synagogue.**
· **Parents give the mass media mixed ratings: some think them a good influence; some, a bad influence; and a sizable number think they have little or no effect on their children.**
· **Parents believe hard rock music to be the least positive influence on their children.**
· **Parents' most persistent worries center on their own success in parenting and on their child's future.**
· **Parents worry more about sons' school performance than about daughters'.**
· **Parents worry more about their daughters' views on sex than about their sons'.**

Chapter 2 described the social context in which young adolescents live, focusing attention on their experiences with school, mass media, church, and peers. In this chapter we describe those same social environments as they look from the parents' perspective.

PARENTS' PERCEPTIONS OF INFLUENCES ON THEIR CHILD

We asked parents to judge the quality of the influence on their child exerted by eleven segments of their environment. The eleven influences and parents' perception of them are given here in order from most to least positive.

Influences	Percent "usually positive" or "very positive"	Percent "usually negative" or "very negative"
Our family life	96	2
My child's teachers	91	2
Church or synagogue	90	1
My child's friends	85	5
Organized sports	72	3
My neighborhood	68	5
Youth organizations (e.g., 4-H, Scouts)	63	3
Television	50	24
Movies	33	14
Hard rock music	10	33

Although we analyzed mothers' and fathers' responses separately, we found no important differences between them in amount of influence they perceived, nor in whether they judged that influence to be positive or negative.

Parents are divided in assessing the influence of mass media.

· Half of parents see TV as a positive influence, while the other half are divided almost equally between rating it as a negative influence or as having little or no influence.
· About one third of parents think movies exert a positive influence; about half think they have little or no influence; and 14 percent say the influence is negative.
· Only 10 percent of parents see hard rock music as a positive influence on their child. More than half think it has little or no influence, and one third think it has a negative influence.

The sex of the child seems relevant in only two influence ratings.

· Perhaps because more boys are involved in organized sports, 79 percent of parents of boys think sports are a positive influence, as compared with 67 percent of parents of girls.
· While 46 percent of the mothers of daughters believe that the church has had a very positive influence, only 40 percent of the mothers of sons see it as a very positive influence.

Parents indicate that the positive effect of five of these influences diminishes as the child progresses from fifth to ninth grade: teachers, the neighborhood, youth organizations, television, and movies. The word from parents on hard rock music is more complicated. The number of parents saying it has little or no influence shrinks by 10 percent between fifth and ninth grade—from 62 percent to 52 percent. At the same time, the number of parents who judge hard rock as having either negative or positive influence increases. Apparently, parents of fifth graders haven't formed strong opinions about hard rock. By ninth grade, many more of them have made up their minds, but they haven't all reached the same conclusion.

PARENTS' CONCERNS AND WORRIES

In Chapter 4, we described young adolescents' worries and compared those ratings with what parents think their child worries about. In a number of instances, parents' estimates fail to match their children's real worries. Often parents miss the reality quite spectacularly. (For data on the following, please refer to Chapter 4: worry about others' use of drugs and alcohol, about hunger and poverty, violence, sexual abuse, nuclear war, being liked by others, and about how the child's friends treat him or her.) Even though they are not accurate at guessing all of what is going on in their children's private thoughts, parents provided us with another glimpse into their view of the child's world when they answered several other questions about their own concerns and worries as parents.

As seems perfectly natural, parents are concerned about how well they are doing as parents and how well their child is being prepared for his or her future. Table 12.1 lists fourteen concerns of parents, in order of the degree of concern indicated by mothers. We find no important distinction between the degrees of concern expressed by mothers and fathers, nor do we find differences in degree of concern according to the grade of the child. Even though we might expect more concern on the part of parents of older children about such matters as drugs and alcohol or the child's view of sex, we discovered no such additional concern.

Table 12.1 Parents' Concerns and Worries

| *Percent responding* very much *or* quite a bit | | |
How much do you worry about . . .	Mother	Father
The job you are doing raising this child	66%	60%
Your child's future	63	66
Your child's happiness	62	62
How your child is doing in school	48	54
Your child's being around drugs and alcohol	46	52
How you and your child feel about each other	37	46
Your child's friends	37	42
How you discipline your child	38	40
The amount of time you spend with your child	36	45
Your child's view of what is right and wrong	35	41
Your child's view of sex	35	36
Your child's eating habits	35	35
Your child's physical health	32	42
Your child's attitude toward authority	31	38

Differences in concern about sons and daughters occur in only two instances. Parents worry more about the school performance of sons than of daughters and more about their daughters' view of sex than about their sons'.

PARENTS' PERCEPTIONS OF THEIR CHILD'S PERSONAL CHARACTERISTICS

In an early part of the survey, we asked parents to rate their child on twenty-four personal characteristics—general helpfulness, concern for others, propensity for getting into trouble, thrift, persistence, level of maturity, and the like. Great diversity in personal characteristics exists among these young adolescents—perhaps even greater diversity than one would find in an adult population of the same size, since to any group's variety of characteristics we must add the variety of growth and development represented in young adolescents. A few generalizations about the way in which people perceive their children are possible.[1]

Both mothers and fathers tend to attribute the following personal characteristics more often to daughters than to sons:

· Excellent student, tries her best at school, seldom gives up without trying
· Goes out of her way to help others, cares about the feelings of others, is concerned about the world
· Never gets into trouble, respects authority
· Mature, involved in many things

Mothers make relatively few distinctions among their child's personal characteristics related to his or her grade, except for these few: More mothers of fifth than of ninth graders state that their child is an excellent student and tries his or her best at school. More mothers of ninth than of fifth graders describe their child as obedient, likely to make his or her own decisions, mature, persistent, and never in trouble.

IMPLICATIONS

When they worry about their children, parents by and large seem to do so without differentiating by sex. But both mothers and fathers do worry more about the school performance of boys than of girls. Does this grow out of the female image of "excellent student, tries her best at school, respects authority, mature," or does it arise from a lingering assumption that boys will have to earn livings and must therefore do their best at school?

Both mothers and fathers worry more about their daughters' view of sex than about sons'. Is this due to the biological fact that girls can become pregnant and boys cannot, or does it mean that parents are holding to an outmoded view of the way things are?

Parents in the throes of seeing their eldest child progress from fifth to ninth grade may take heart from the content of the description that tends to characterize ninth graders more than any other age—that they are obedient, mature, persistent, not in trouble. Truly, life in many families does improve, grow calmer, increase in predictability, when the child has successfully passed into the eighth and ninth grades. By that time, children have frequently developed more serviceable social skills and are more comfortable with themselves, even though they may appear to be less motivated to do extremely well at school.

CHAPTER 13

Parents' Values and Moral Standards

· **Fathers and mothers agree that their most desired goal is "to have a happy family life."**
· **In general, mothers and fathers have similar value priorities.**
· **More mothers than fathers rank "to have God at the center of my life" as a top value.**
· **More fathers than mothers rank "to be successful" as one of their top values.**
· **The values of parents and their children, though similarities can be found, show more differences than similarities.**

Popular wisdom would have it that the values of today's children and of their parents are worlds apart. It's hard to test a theory like that informally, since casual conversation about the children of one's friends and acquaintances tends to yield conflicting information. Researchers have seldom had the opportunity this study affords to examine parent and child values as they do in fact exist. Chapters 5 and 6 presented findings on the values and moral beliefs of young adolescents. This chapter concentrates on the values and moral beliefs of parents but also points out some comparisons between the values and beliefs of youth and their parents.

PARENTS' VALUES

The survey asked parents to express their preferences for sixteen value statements, prefaced by the following instructions:

What do you want in life? For the item below, indicate how much you want each one. Your choices are:

At the top of my list: This is one of the 3 or 4 things I want most in life.

Very much: I want this very much.

Quite a bit: I want this quite a bit.

Somewhat: I want this some.

Very little or not at all: I don't want this much at all.

Table 13.1 presents the sixteen ranked value items, listed in descending order of their value as ranked by mothers. It also gives means for fathers and mothers and the percentage of each parent group placing each statement in the "top of my list" category.

Table 13.1   Parents' Ranking of Values

Value	Means		Percent ranked "at the top of my list"	
	Mothers	Fathers	Mothers	Fathers
To have a happy family life	4.75	4.60	79	67
To be a good parent	4.65	4.41	70	50
To have wisdom	4.19	4.06	35	28
To have God at the center of my life	4.18	3.76	55	39
To be able to forgive others	4.09	3.82	30	20
To feel good about myself	4.07	3.91	28	21
To live responsibly toward others	3.94	3.78	18	13
To have friends I can count on	3.67	3.56	12	9
To do things that help people	3.63	3.49	11	9
To do something important with my life	3.61	3.65	18	17
To have a world without hunger or poverty	3.60	3.28	15	10
To be successful	3.18	3.57	9	14
To have lots of fun and good times	2.71	2.91	3	4
To have lots of money	2.38	2.66	3	5
To do whatever I want to do, when I want to do it	2.07	2.35	2	3
To have influence and authority over others	2.01	2.28	1	1

Both mothers and fathers rank "to have a happy family life" as their most desired goal. Seventy-nine percent of mothers select this goal as one of the three or four things they want most in life, and another 18 percent say they want it "very much." Sixty-seven percent of fathers include this goal in their "top of the list" category, with an additional 29 percent wanting it "very much."

Ranked second and close to happy family life is a related value, "to be a good parent," also placed in the "top of my list" category by over half of both mothers and fathers.

One or two differences are apparent when we compare mothers and fathers in their ranking of these values. Mothers put more values in their "top of list" category than do fathers. When asked to place three or four statements in the "top of my list" category, mothers place an average of four choices there, while fathers place an average of three.

We see that mothers have higher mean scores than fathers for each of the nine top-ranked values, and fathers tend to place more importance on six of the seven lowest-ranked values—values that emphasize success, money, good times, and influence over others. More agreement occurs among mothers than among fathers on their order of preference.

HEDONIST OR PEOPLE-ORIENTED?

The value preferences of parents tend to group in clusters or patterns. We identified two of these clusters for further analysis; one of them we call a hedonistic value orientation and another we call a people-oriented value orientation. The hedonist value orientation includes three values: (1) to have lots of fun and good times, (2) to have lots of money, and (3) to do whatever I want to do, when I want to do it. We learned that people with high preference for these three value statements also have the following characteristics: (a) a strong positive association with values of success and authority over others, (b) an association with a hedonistic value orientation in their spouse, and (c) a negative association with strong religious beliefs and practices.

The people-oriented value orientation combined these three value statements: (1) to do things that help people, (2) to have a world without hunger or poverty, and (3) to live responsibly toward others. These people-oriented preferences, strongly associated with each other, are also associated for both mothers and fathers with a number of other values (listed here in order of the mathematical strength of their relationships with the three people-oriented items):

To be able to forgive others
To have God at the center of my life
To have wisdom
To do something important with my life
To feel good about myself

In addition, we find that parents who put strong emphasis on the people-oriented values also tend to have higher scores on religious beliefs and behavior.

YOUTH AND PARENT VALUES COMPARED

One of our major reasons for asking parents about their goals in life was to compare them with their children's life goals, described in Chapter 6. Ten items on each list given to parents and children were identical, so we can compare them (see Table 13.2).

Table 13.2   Comparison of Youth and Parent Values

Value	*Means*		*Means*	
	Mothers	Fathers	Daughters	Sons
To have a happy family life	4.75	4.60	4.33	4.12
To have God at the center of my life	4.18	3.76	3.94	3.83
To feel good about myself	4.07	3.91	4.04	3.89
To have friends I can count on	3.67	3.56	4.10	3.89
To do things that help people	3.63	3.49	3.56	3.38
To do something important with my life	3.61	3.65	4.19	4.00
To have a world without hunger or poverty	3.60	3.28	3.88	3.72
To have lots of fun and good times	2.71	2.91	3.86	3.75
To have lots of money	2.38	2.66	3.11	3.37
To do whatever I want to do, when I want to do it	2.07	2.35	2.75	2.96

The absolute values of the means for parents and youth are not fully comparable, however, because youth were asked to select their three or four choices at the "top of my list" from a group of twenty-four items, while parents worked with only sixteen. Nevertheless, we can make several observations about the comparisons.

· Parents rank two values ("to have a happy family life" and "to have God at the center of my life") higher than youth, and on two values ("to feel good about myself" and "to do things that help people") parents and youth are about the same.

· Having a happy family life is given a higher mean rating by parents than by youth, but it is the top value for both.

Youth rank six of the ten values higher than parents. They are listed below, in the order in which youth value them, together with the difference between youth and parent mean ratings.

Value	Youth Mean	Parent Mean	Difference
To do something important with my life	4.10	3.63	.53
To have friends I can count on	4.00	3.61	.40
To have lots of fun and good times	3.81	2.81	1.00
To have a world without hunger and poverty	3.80	3.44	.36
To have lots of money	3.24	2.52	.72
To do what I want to do, when I want to do it	2.85	2.21	.64

The stronger hedonistic values of youth (fun, money, freedom) may not surprise readers, but the others on this list might. Youth are concerned about their future achievement and having solid friendships. In addition, they are more concerned about hunger and poverty than are their parents.

PARENTS' MORAL BELIEFS

Parents' ideas about right and wrong are measured on a five-item moral beliefs scale; four of the five are identical to items asked of youth. We asked parents to indicate how wrong or how right behaviors of young adolescents were in the following moral situations: (Their options for response were "very right," "right," "I'm not sure," "wrong," and "very wrong.")

a. Tracy thinks that shoplifting from a big store is not so bad because "they'll never miss it." She steals a $25 radio from a large department store. How right or wrong is it for her to steal the radio?

b. Gary is 12. His parents expect him to do his homework. Sometimes he lies to his parents and tells them he has done his homework when he really hasn't. He does this so that his parents won't keep asking him about his homework. How right or wrong is Gary to lie to his parents?

c. Alice, who is 15, didn't think she would get pregnant, but the doctor said she was. She decided she did not want to have the baby, so she went to another doctor and had an abortion. How right or wrong was it for her to have this abortion?

d. Jim is 13. Sometimes he and his friends get together and drink a couple of cans of beer. How right or wrong are they to do this?

e. (*Not included in the young adolescents' survey.*) Tom and Sue are fifteen. They have known each other for two years and have been going steady for several months. They say they love each other. Sometimes, now, they "go all the way," that is, have sexual intercourse. How right or wrong is it for them to have sexual intercourse?

The following presents parents' views on these questions as compared with their children's responses.

Percent saying "very wrong"

	Mothers	Daughters	Fathers	Sons
Shoplifting	93	91	91	79
Lying to parents	73	48	70	41
Teenage beer drinking	67	52	53	41
Teenage abortion	41	33	37	29
Teenage sexual intercourse (not asked on youth survey)	71	—	59	—

- Except in the case of abortion, where opinion is divided, the majority of parents clearly consider these behaviors to be very wrong for young adolescents.
- Although both parents consider beer drinking and sexual intercourse by young adolescents to be wrong, more mothers than fathers consider these behaviors to be "very wrong."
- Comparing the moral beliefs of parents and youth reveals only one similarity: daughters are similar to parents in that 91 percent consider shoplifting to be "very wrong." On the rest of the compared items, parents indicate stronger disapproval than youth.
- Fathers and daughters are fairly close in the percent who think abortion and teenage beer drinking are "very wrong." The greatest disparity is between moral views of mothers and sons.

Differences could be found among parents of children in different school grades on only two items: (1) on teenage beer drinking, the rate of "very wrong" increases from 48 percent of fathers of a fifth-grade child to 56 percent of fathers of a ninth-grade child; (2) on teenage intercourse, the rating of "very wrong" increases from 52 percent of fathers of a fifth-grade child to 64 percent of fathers of a ninth-grade child. The "very wrong" rating on teenage intercourse increases from 68 percent of mothers of a fifth-grade child to 74 percent of mothers of a ninth-grade child.

Surprisingly, we found no other differences related to grade of child on the other three moral value situations or on any of the sixteen value preferences of parents. Even more remarkable, we are unable to find any evidence that the moral beliefs and value preferences of parents relate in any way to the sex of their child.

SUMMARY

In general, fathers and mothers have similar values and moral beliefs and even prioritize them similarly. Children and parents, however, show some similarities and some differences in choosing values. Some of the differences are easily understandable—a result, no doubt, of the gap between the ages of parents and their children.

The responses of children and their parents come close to agreement regarding specific actions related to morality that they may have discussed at home. The differences are visible mostly in the differing degrees of wrongness they attribute to the actions.

From much of the data reported in this chapter, parental standards appear to be higher than those of their children, with some exceptions. The idealism of youth is evident in their desire to do something important with their lives and to inhabit a world where hunger and poverty no longer exist. They also more strongly oppose racial segregation than do their parents. These exceptions suggest that the young are still in touch with being powerless and therefore champion the cause of other powerless groups. Perhaps parents can learn from their children in this area.

CHAPTER 14

Parents' Religious Beliefs
and Social Attitudes

· **More fathers and sons support expenditures for nuclear weapons than do mothers and daughters, but no more than 19 percent of any category expresses such support.**
· **Ninety-seven percent of parents surveyed claim membership in a church or synagogue.**
· **Children of parents who are racially prejudiced tend to echo those prejudiced attitudes.**
· **A majority of parents support the idea of male and female equality.**
· **Ninety-three percent of parents believe sexual intercourse for fifteen-year-olds to be "wrong" or "very wrong."**
· **A number of parents' religious, social, and political attitudes are mirrored in the attitudes of their child.**

Emerson said it in a sentence: "Thought is the seed of action." Our thoughts, our attitudes, our beliefs play important roles in shaping us. But for parents, the crucial (though often unspoken) question is, How well do we transmit our attitudes and beliefs to our children? In this chapter we discuss some parental patterns of belief and attitude and show that some of these patterns do, indeed, influence the thinking and behavior of their children.

POLITICAL ATTITUDES

About 40 percent of these parents identify themselves as Republicans and 33 percent as Democrats. About half of them describe their political beliefs as moderate, or at the middle of the political spectrum. Of the other half, 9 percent describe their political beliefs as liberal, and 41 percent describe their political beliefs as conservative.

Both the parent survey and the youth survey included questions about government action. Responses reveal one difference in viewpoint between the generations and one similarity. We asked respondents to express their degree of agreement with these two statements: "Our government should do more to help people who are poor and hungry" and "Our country should spend more money for nuclear weapons."

While 50 percent of parents agree with the first statement, 86 percent of young adolescents support that view. On the second statement, young adolescents and their parents more closely agree: almost the same number of young people (12 percent) as parents (10 percent) endorse more spending for nuclear weapons, while 65 percent of youth and 66 percent of parents do not. Boys (19 percent) and fathers (14 percent) are more likely than mothers (6 percent) and girls (5 percent) to support more spending for nuclear weapons.

The responses of *all* youth and *all* parents provided the data for the analysis just given. We further analyzed the data, including only those children whose parents also took the survey.[1] With this group of parents and children, we found that parents tend to agree with each other on the two questions, and that a modest but significant relationship exists between the attitudes of parents and their children on the two issues.

THE IMPORTANCE OF RELIGION

Nearly all of the parents—98 percent of mothers and 96 percent of fathers—who participated in this study are members of an organized religious group. This is a likely finding, since it was through their child's participation in a program associated with a church that most of the parents were invited to take the survey.

About half of these parents identify themselves as either extremely active or very active participants in the life of their religious group.

Our survey inquired into the importance of religion and the church to parents, as we did with the young adolescents, by asking the following questions:

How important is your church or synagogue to you?

	Mothers	*Fathers*
Percent answering		
Extremely important	33	26
Very important	46	42
Somewhat important	17	22
Slightly important	3	7
Not important	1	3

Overall, how important is religion in your life?

	Mothers	*Fathers*
The most important influence in my life	36	26
One of the most important influences	44	41
A somewhat important influence	18	26
One of the least important influences	2	7

Responses to the two questions are similar. If we combine the first two categories of response for each of these two questions, we can see that membership in a religious organization is of significant importance to about three quarters of mothers and about two thirds of fathers.

We asked their children about another element of behavior connected with the importance of religion—conversation at home about religious matters.

How often does your family sit down together and talk about God, the Bible, or other religious things?

	5th	*6th*	*7th*	*8th*	*9th*
Percent who respond "once a week or more"	30	28	24	22	21

As this response makes evident,

· Many adults who are active in group religious life nevertheless do not often discuss religious matters in their own homes.
· The frequency with which families discuss religious matters appears to decrease as the child moves from fifth to ninth grade.

This last point deserves emphasis, particularly for those who are concerned with the transfer of religious attitudes and values. As was pointed out in Chapter 2, the two items in the entire survey most closely connected with young people who hold favorable attitudes toward the church are parents who consider religion important and, further, who talk about religion at home. Of the two, talking about religion at home is the more powerful influence on children's attitudes toward the church.

PARENTS' RACIAL PREJUDICE

Two statements in the parent survey probed the attitude of parents toward people of other races. They are listed below, together with the percentage of parents who showed evidence of prejudice by responding in agreement with the statement.

	Percent who agree	
	Mothers	*Fathers*
I don't trust people of other races.	4	6
I think it is wrong for a boy and a girl of different races to date each other.	46	50

The following situation was also given to parents to assess their attitude:

The Olsons are a white family who live in a neighborhood of mostly white people. A black family is considering buying a house nearby. The Olsons are trying to stop the black family from moving in. How right or wrong is it for the Olsons to do this?

Four percent of mothers and 6 percent of fathers believed the Olsons were right in their actions.

From the responses we learned that more than 80 percent of both parent samples disagree with the statement, "I don't trust people of other races." Parents are divided on the propriety of interracial dating, with about 48 percent disapproving and about 20 percent not sure.

We also discovered that parents who have either very high or very low scores on these questions tend to have a spouse who shares their attitudes, and that children of prejudiced parents are likely to be similarly prejudiced.[2]

PARENT ATTITUDES ON SEX ROLES AND IDENTITY

A continuing controversy goes on in our society over the proper roles of males and females at work as well as in the home. Because the topic of sexism is at the forefront of present-day thought, it becomes important to know the attitudes of the parents of young people whose identities are now being formed. We asked parents to express themselves on nine questions having to do with sex roles and identity. Their responses appear in Table 14.1.

Table 14.1   Parent Attitudes: Sex Roles and Identity

		Strongly Disagree	Disagree	Not Sure	Agree	Strongly Agree
A young child is better off if his or her mother doesn't work outside the home.	Mothers	4%	18%	17%	33%	29%
	Fathers	2%	12%	14%	36%	36%
Women can handle pressure as well as men when making a decision.	Mothers	1%	7%	10%	47%	35%
	Fathers	2%	19%	15%	47%	17%
I think boys should grow up being just as gentle and caring as girls.	Mothers	1%	5%	5%	54%	35%
	Fathers	2%	15%	11%	55%	17%
Even if they have families, women should be given opportunities equal to men to work and have careers outside the home.	Mothers	3%	12%	13%	49%	23%
	Fathers	5%	19%	13%	49%	14%
I think boys and girls should be raised very differently from each other.	Mothers	24%	59%	9%	7%	1%
	Fathers	12%	57%	14%	15%	2%
I think men should have more freedom than women.	Mothers	47%	47%	4%	2%	1%
	Fathers	21%	63%	8%	8%	1%
Mothers and fathers should play an equal role in caring for children, even if it means taking some time away from their jobs.	Mothers	2%	22%	13%	41%	22%
	Fathers	2%	24%	14%	44%	15%

		Strongly Disagree	*Disagree*	*Not Sure*	*Agree*	*Strongly Agree*
I think women should have all the same rights as men.	Mothers	3%	18%	15%	42%	23%
	Fathers	2%	14%	11%	53%	19%
I think the father should make all the important decisions in a family.	Mothers	27%	51%	5%	12%	4%
	Fathers	16%	59%	8%	13%	3%

When we combine the responses of mothers and fathers, we find that 58 percent of parents support equality between the sexes and 31 percent favor inequality. We find further that mothers are slightly more supportive of equality between the sexes than fathers, but that fathers' and mothers' views are, in general, quite similar, and that mothers who hold traditional views about sex roles tend to have children who also hold traditional views.[3]

Parents holding sexist views also tend to have the following characteristics when compared with parents who hold less sexist views:[4]

· stronger racial prejudice
· lower scores on a measure of horizontal religion
· higher scores on a measure of restricting religion
· mother less educated than mothers holding less sexist views
· tendency to consider religion very important

PARENT ATTITUDES: ADOLESCENT SEXUAL BEHAVIOR

Two questions explored parental attitudes toward teens' sexual behavior. One asked for their approval or disapproval of a situation in which two fifteen-year-olds who are going steady decide to have sexual intercourse. The second asked them to agree or disagree with the statement, "I think young people should be able to experiment with sexual intercourse before marriage." The findings from these two questions lead to the following conclusions:

· The overwhelming majority of parents—95 percent of mothers and 91 percent of fathers—consider it wrong for steady-dating fifteen-year-old couples to have sexual intercourse.
· Eighty-five percent of mothers and 79 percent of fathers believe that young people should not experiment with sexual intercourse before marriage.
· On both questions, parents of ninth graders express stronger disapproval

of premarital intercourse than do parents of youth in lower grades. Perhaps what was formerly a hypothetical and general question becomes real and personal when one has a child in the early teens, and some minds change.

· An attitude of sexual permissiveness is inversely related to religious measures for both parents and, to a slightly lesser degree, for their children, as well.[5]

· Sexual permissiveness tends to be positively related to liberal political views and approval of male-female equality.[6]

SUMMARY

We discover from much of the foregoing that spouses tend to share attitudes, particularly social attitudes. Whether this comes about as the result of long-term influence by one partner on the other, or whether marriage partners choose one another in part on the basis of shared attitudes, these data do not tell us.[7] But this study provides strong evidence that spouses' attitudes tend to match rather than differ on political position, the extremes of racial prejudice, attitudes toward sex roles, and the degree of sexual permissiveness appropriate for teenagers.

A question of considerable importance to all adults who deal with young adolescents is whether, in fact, some of their influence "rubs off" on the young people with whom they deal.

We find that influence does appear to "rub off." The powerful connection between parents' conversation about religion at home and the positive attitude of their children toward the church is only one evidence of it. We find, in these data, considerable evidence of parental influence on the beliefs and social attitudes of their children. The listing below gives the correlations, ranked in order from high to low, between the characteristics of young adolescents and of their parents. Correlation is a mathematical means of indicating the strength of the relationship between two things, of expressing the likelihood that where one factor exists the other also exists. The higher the number, the more the child and parent have in common on that issue.[8] For example, the first item on the list says that if the mother has a positive attitude toward the church it is likely that her children will. It also tells us that if the father has a positive attitude toward the church it is even more likely that his children will have positive feelings about the church.

	Mother-child correlation	Father-child correlation
Positive attitude toward church	.33	.37
Frequency of prayer	.28	.27
Horizontal religion	.26	.26
Racial prejudice	.26	.21
Sexism	.21	.14
Liberating religion	.17	.18
Restricting religion	.14	.13
Acceptance of traditional moral values	.11	.13
More government spending for the poor	.12	.11
More government spending for military	.12	.11
Hedonistic value orientation	.11	.11

In sum, then, we find that what youth value and believe are in part transmitted through the values and beliefs of their parents.[9]

CHAPTER 15

Family Dynamics

- Most parents surveyed think husbands and wives should share family responsibilities and have equal access to career development, but in the vast majority of households, labor is divided along traditional lines, with women doing most or all of the housework and men doing most or all of the repair work.
- Nearly three quarters of young adolescents report, "There is a lot of love in my family."
- Mothers tend to give affection equally to sons and daughters. Fathers tend to give more affection to daughters than to sons.
- Girls receive more nurturance from parents than do boys.
- More parents discipline inductively than by love withdrawal or coercion.
- The potential for physical abuse of children decreases rapidly between fifth grade and ninth grade as physical punishment becomes less frequent.
- Spouses who are physically violent with one another are also likely to use coercive discipline and to abuse their children.

Perhaps no segment of a young adolescent's life is more hidden from outside observation than that portion of time spent with the family. And yet family life may be the most powerful influence in shaping a young person's personality, values, and assumptions about the world. We need to know how family members communicate with one another, how they assign power and responsibility, what assumptions they make about the value of each family member, and what methods they use to control and discipline children if we are to understand the world of the young adolescent.

Because of the unique structure of this study, which allowed us to question the young adolescent as well as the parent or parents, we have an unusual window on what goes on in the homes of several thousand young adolescents and on how family atmosphere affects them.

Answers to our questions told us something about how roles and tasks are assigned in the family, about the quality of time parents and children spend together, about the style of parenting employed, and about the occurrences of unreasonable pressure, abuse, and violence that children of some families have experienced.

FAMILY ROLES, TASKS, AND TIME

The majority of parents in this study affirm the belief that women should be able to work outside the home, even when they have children, and that fathers should take a role equal to mothers in caring for children. They also reject the notion that fathers should make all the important decisions in the family. (See Table 14.1, especially the last three questions.) In order to test this ideal against reality, we asked both mothers and fathers about the division of labor in their household. The results from all households in which both parents took the survey are shown below.

	Percent who report that:	
Jobs	*I do all or most*	*I share equally with partner*
Cleaning our house or apartment		
Mothers	89	9
Fathers	5	15
Cooking meals		
Mothers	90	7
Fathers	5	10
Disciplining the children		
Mothers	35	61
Fathers	14	72
Washing the children's clothes		
Mothers	93	5
Fathers	5	7
Grocery shopping		
Mothers	82	13
Fathers	8	21
Repairing things around the house		
Mothers	9	17
Fathers	86	10

These figures outline something of a gap between the ideal and the real. The division of labor in these households is quite traditional, women taking charge of the lion's share of the household tasks except for repair. Discipline is the only task on which mothers and fathers appear to share responsibility fairly equally. Despite what parents affirm about the desirability of equal division of labor, the example that young adolescents are seeing played out in their homes is a traditional one.

Another important factor to examine in studying family dynamics is the amount and quality of time parents spend with their children. The popular image would have the successful business executive rush off to important meetings from dawn until dark, leaving little time for either spouse or children. To test this image we asked: "How much time does your family (parents and children living at home) spend doing things together during an average week?"

Responses	*Percent of mothers*	*Percent of fathers*
None—someone is always off doing something else	3	3
1–5 hours	31	35
5–10 hours	30	33
11–20 hours	23	20
21 or more hours	13	9

Parents' responses draw a somewhat more positive picture, showing remarkable agreement between fathers and mothers, who were requested, of course, not to communicate with each other about their responses.

A majority of parents report a weekly total of between five and ten hours spent with the family. We found further that the amount of time a family spends together is based more on the patterns of interaction the family develops than on the age of the child.

In order to determine the amount of high-quality time spent with the young adolescent, we asked two similarly-worded questions: "During an average day, how much time does your mother (father) spend alone with you doing things like talking, playing, or just being together?" Their responses follow.

	Less than 5 minutes	*5–30 minutes*	*30 minutes to 1 hour*	*1–2 hours*	*3–4 hours*
Percent of girls with mothers	12	29	24	19	15
Percent of boys with mothers	11	29	23	20	17
Percent of girls with fathers	19	32	22	15	11
Percent of boys with fathers	14	28	24	19	15

The majority of young adolescents report receiving an hour or less of one-to-one time with each parent. Girls and boys receive equal time with mothers; fathers appear to spend slightly less time, on the average, with daughters than with sons.

PARENTING STYLES

If time spent with a child is important, the kind of atmosphere that a child experiences and associates with home is even more important. To determine the kind of atmosphere young adolescents live in, we included in the youth and parent surveys a number of questions related to four important dimensions of parenting: demonstration of parental affection, parental nurturance, parental control, and discipline.

PARENTAL AFFECTION

We asked young adolescents about two kinds of demonstrative affection—physical (hugging and kissing) and verbal ("I love you," "I'm proud of you"). As the percentages below indicate, most young adolescents experience frequent expressions of affection.

	Percent daily	*Percent a couple of times a week*
How often does your mother hug or kiss you or just put her arms around you?	59	21
How often does your father hug or kiss you or just put his arms around you?	39	23
How often does your mother say things to you like "I love you" or "I'm proud of you"?	45	32
How often does your father say things to you like "I love you" or "I'm proud of you"?	34	30

Youth report less demonstrative affection from fathers than from mothers, as many other family studies find. What is particularly interesting is that affection is related to grade in school and sex of child, as shown in Figure 41. We find that female family members both give and receive more affection than males.

· Both boys and girls receive more affection from mothers than fathers.
· Girls receive more affection from both fathers and mothers than do boys.
· While both boys and girls report a decline in affection between fifth and ninth grade, the greatest decline is in affection from fathers.[1]

Although the patterns shown in Figure 41 are based on information provided by young adolescents, these patterns were corroborated by other information provided by mothers and fathers.

''LOVE IN THE FAMILY''

We asked all three groups (young adolescents, mothers, fathers) for reactions to the statement, ''There is a lot of love in my family.'' Here are their responses.

	Young Adolescents	Mothers	Fathers
Percent who say			
Not at all true	5	1	1
Slightly true	9	1	2
Somewhat true	13	10	13
Quite true	28	35	42
Very true	46	53	43

All three groups choose the response ''very true'' or ''quite true'' most often, but young adolescents, more than parents, report a lack of love. When looking at an index of family closeness that combines parents' and young adolescents' views of how much love there is in the family, plus their estimates of how well family members get along with each other, we find that a slight decline in family closeness occurs between fifth and ninth grade and that girls report slightly more family closeness than do boys.

NURTURANCE

Parental nurturance includes a number of behaviors such as being available to help when a problem arises, listening to a child's concerns, helping the child feel cared about, and providing support and encouragement. We asked a set of ten questions about things mothers and fathers might do to provide nurturance. On each of the items taken individually, more than half of all adolescents say

Figure 41   Demonstrative Affection from Mothers and Fathers

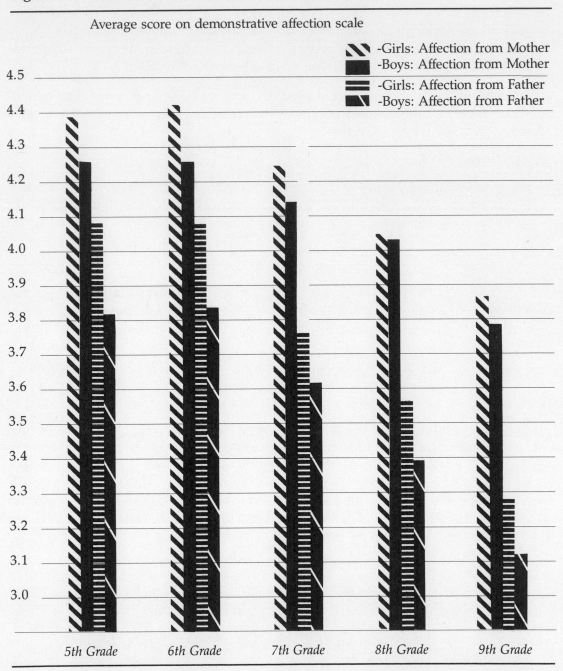

Average score on demonstrative affection scale

-Girls: Affection from Mother
-Boys: Affection from Mother
-Girls: Affection from Father
-Boys: Affection from Father

5th Grade   6th Grade   7th Grade   8th Grade   9th Grade

their parents are nurturing. Responses to two of the questions, by way of example, follow.

	Percent never	Percent once in a while	Percent sometimes	Percent often true	Percent very often true
My mother tries to help me feel better when I am upset or scared.	4	9	13	25	50
My father tries to help me feel better when I am upset or scared.	8	16	20	25	31

In analyzing all ten questions, we find patterns much like those reported for affection:[2]

· Young adolescents receive more nurturance from mothers than from fathers.
· Girls receive more nurturance from both parents than do boys.
· Nurturance from both parents declines with grade, for both boys and girls.

While most young adolescents experience relatively high levels of affection and nurturance, these two parenting behaviors decrease between the fifth and ninth grades. This decrease in affection and nurturance comes at a very critical time. As young adolescents move from fifth to ninth grade, their need to establish a positive self-concept increases. At the same time, they may experience increased threats to their self-esteem. All signs point to the need for more parental nurturance and affection at this period of life, rather than less.

The young adolescent may find it necessary to seek affection and nurturance more from his or her friends. Such a process is not entirely undesirable, of course, for it forces a young adolescent to learn how to establish the kinds of relationships that generate support and esteem—part of gaining lifelong skills in social competence.

PARENTAL CONTROL

One of the most important tasks of parenting is to establish rules or boundaries for behavior. In doing this, parents usually choose one of three major control styles to determine, modify, and discuss the child's obligations and responsibilities.[3]

The *authoritarian approach* is nondemocratic, nonnegotiable, and inflexible. The parent makes rules, tolerates little deviation from these rules, and is firm and swift with punishment.

The *democratic approach* is used by parents who seek to establish rule and behavioral guidelines in concert with the child. The parent seeks the child's advice and input and then firmly explains in a rational way what the agreed-upon rules are and what the consequences are for rule violations.

The *permissive approach* is quite casual. The parent does not set particular rules, monitor behavior, or punish, and allows the child to find boundaries and limits mostly on his or her own.

In most homes, even though there are probably times when each of the three styles operates, one style usually predominates. Groups of questions were developed to assess each of these control styles:

Youth's view of mother's
        democratic control
        authoritarian control
        permissive control
Mother's view of her own
        democratic control
        authoritarian control
        permissive control
Youth's view of father's
        democratic control
        authoritarian control
        permissive control
Father's view of his own
        democratic control
        authoritarian control
        permissive control

We find, fortunately, some degree of correspondence between the views of parents and children on the type of control used in their home.[4] For example, when a youth reports that mother is high in authoritarian control, the mother tends also to report herself as using authoritarian control.

We made four important discoveries about how parents exercise control:

· Democratic control is the most frequently used style. Parents use authoritarian and permissive styles less frequently, each being used by about 15 to 20 percent of parents.
· Mothers use democratic control more often than fathers; fathers use authoritarian control more than do mothers; mothers and fathers do not differ on the frequency with which they use permissive control.

· Young adolescents report that democratic control declines slightly between the fifth and ninth grades, and that authoritarian control increases. Parents see exactly the reverse. One explanation for the perceptual difference is that some young adolescents may come to see any kind of control as noxious and interpret it as nondemocratic and authoritarian.

· Boys report more authoritarian control from mothers than do girls, while boys and girls report the same amount of authoritarian control by fathers.

DISCIPLINE

Control style describes a general atmosphere in the home; discipline is the method parents use when rules or behavioral standards are violated. Parents normally choose one of three major kinds of discipline.

In *coercive discipline*, the parent seeks to control the child by capitalizing on his or her own physical or psychological power. The parent may strike the child or threaten to do so, yell or scream at the child, or deprive the child of something he or she wants in order to coerce the child into obedience.

Love withdrawal refers to parental behaviors that manipulate the child, like pouting, expressing disappointment, avoiding the child, or giving the child the "silent treatment."

Inductive discipline relies on explanation and discussion. The parent attempts to explain to the child, on rational grounds, why he or she should behave differently. The explanation deals with the importance of a particular rule, why breaking it is undesirable, how violating a rule conflicts with the child's concern for other people and their welfare, or how it can endanger the child himself or herself.

The advantage of coercive discipline is that it usually produces immediate results, and that is no doubt why so many parents continue to employ it. The disadvantage is that it has negative long-term results, and adults who grew up under a mostly coercive discipline style know them well—the tendency to lie to parents or to tell half-truths, the tendency to hide their real behavior and to invent plausible "cover stories."

The advantage of induction is that it appeals to a child's own internal resources for controlling and monitoring behavior, as opposed to coercion and love withdrawal, which function to create fear of punishment by external forces. When parents depend solely on coercion or love withdrawal, their children will frequently become clever enough to break rules in situations where parents will not find out. Adults who choose induction believe that this method will create internal standards in a child that affect behavior whether or not the parent knows about the behavior.[5]

We asked groups of questions intended to measure each of these from both the young adolescents' and parents' points of view.

Three kinds of coercive discipline are listed below, with the percentages of youth who report experiencing each form when "I do something wrong."

	My Mother	My Father
Parent slaps or hits me.		
Percent of young adolescents who respond,		
Never	48	52
Once in a while	30	24
Sometimes	13	13
Often or very often	9	10
Parent yells or shouts at me.		
Percent of young adolescents who respond,		
Never	11	18
Once in a while	31	30
Sometimes	30	27
Often or very often	29	25
Parents make me stay in the house and won't let me be with my friends.		
Percent of young adolescents who respond,		
Never	22	28
Once in a while	30	29
Sometimes	27	24
Often or very often	20	19

About 30 percent of young adolescents report that parents withdraw love "often" or "very often" "when I do something wrong," demonstrating disapproval by acting cold and unfriendly or by giving the child the "silent treatment."

Of the three types of discipline, young adolescents report more inductive techniques than either love withdrawal or coercion. About 50 percent say their mothers, and about 45 percent say their fathers, use inductive discipline. Inductive discipline includes a parent's sitting down with the child to "have a long talk about why it is important to obey" a particular rule, explaining "how this disobedience hurts me," and trying to find out why the child thought the rule infraction was okay.

The use of both coercive discipline and inductive discipline decline slightly with grade level, while rates of love withdrawal remain stable.[6] This suggests that parents do less disciplining as the young adolescent advances in grade.

Further evidence of this is the grade-by-grade decline in the percentage of young adolescents who report "I always get punished when I disobey my parents (or parent)." Boys are subjected to more coercive discipline than girls.[7]

Beyond control styles and methods of discipline, another element has the potential for influence on the young person: pressure to excel. However, parents differ on this point. Exerting pressure is usually a conscious and intended act, and many people think it has positive results.

In order to test the degree of parental pressure to achieve, we asked young adolescents to respond to two similar questions:

	5th	6th	7th	8th	9th
My mother keeps pushing me to do my best in whatever I do.					
Percent who respond "very often true" or "often true"					
Boys	60	66	67	69	66
Girls	51	58	62	63	67
My father keeps pushing me to do my best in whatever I do.					
Percent who respond "very often true" or "often true"					
Boys	56	60	62	61	61
Girls	47	48	55	56	54

Generally speaking, young adolescents who say their parents push them to do their best believe that they are acting in the young person's own best interest. "My parents push me" responses are related to several positive circumstances: parental expressions of affection, inductive discipline, and democratic control.

Another question asked the young person whether the pressure from parents was reasonable. The statement, "My parents expect too much of me," was made and respondents invited to agree or disagree. Nineteen percent of boys and 16 percent of girls agreed. This question marks the dividing line between the kind of parental expectation that is generally viewed by the child as encouragement and the expectation that children see as unreasonable pressure.

This smaller group of youth who say their parents expect too much tend to report that their parents

—exercise authoritarian control
—use coercive discipline
—employ love withdrawal
—sometimes physically abuse them

They also report

—lying to parents
—conflict with parents
—strong peer influence
—negative peer pressure
—worry that they might kill themselves
—influence by the mass media

Among this group we also find a negative association with

—parental nurturance
—democratic controls
—parental trust
—family closeness
—high self-esteem
—positive school climate
—parental harmony
—achievement motivation
—time spent daily with mother

One could scarcely invent a list that more powerfully illustrates the potential dangers that accompany unreasonably high expectations for a child's achievement. The data do not, however, resolve the question of whether the parental expectations were ever at any time reasonable. What the data outline is a pitched battle—parents and young persons using the weapons at their disposal to cause as much hurt and frustration to the other as possible—all of it self-defeating and without hope unless somehow the cycle of conflict is broken.

ABUSE OF CHILD

The dark picture just drawn of unreasonable pressure on children and the behaviors related to it leads us to yet another difficult subject—control of young adolescents by physical means and by abuse. Three survey questions shed some light on this issue. The first looks at how much youth worry about abuse.

	5th	6th	7th	8th	9th

I worry that one of my parents will hit me so hard that I will be badly hurt.

Percent who say they worry about this "very much" or "quite a bit"

	5th	6th	7th	8th	9th
Boys	20	13	15	10	9
Girls	15	12	10	8	8

A surprising number of young adolescents express this worry, particularly those in the earlier grades, and particularly boys.

Parents were asked questions about hitting or slapping their child and about how often they become angry and potentially violent toward their child.

How many times in the past year would you say you spanked, hit, slapped, or otherwise put a hand to your child?

	5th	6th	7th	8th	9th

Percent who say they spank, hit, etc. three or more times in the past year

	5th	6th	7th	8th	9th
Mothers	57	46	39	31	22
Fathers	46	40	30	26	19

How often do you get so angry at your child that you are afraid you might hurt him or her?

	5th	6th	7th	8th	9th

Percent who say they get angry enough to hurt "once in a while," "sometimes," "often," or "very often"

	5th	6th	7th	8th	9th
Mothers	38	34	31	31	28
Fathers	37	36	33	31	32

Youth in younger grades, and especially boys, are more likely to be in danger of physical punishment from a parent, and from mothers more than fathers.

The responses to these three questions are summarized in Figure 42, a physical abuse index, which shows the steady decline in parental physical punishment of the child between fifth and ninth grade.

Figure 42 Physical Abuse Index by Grade

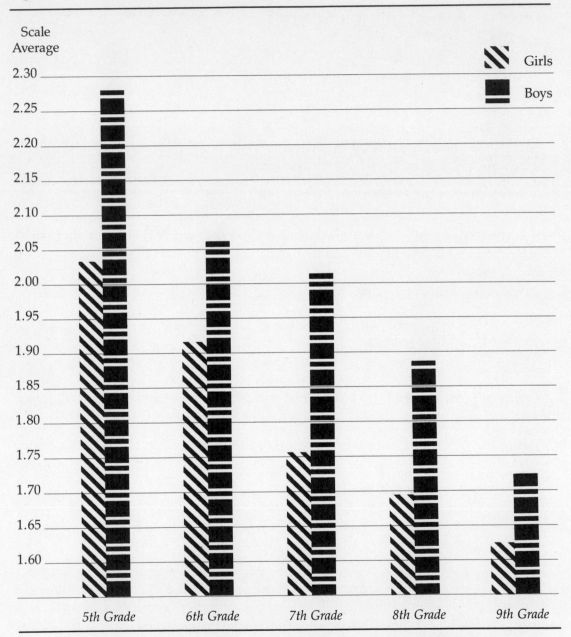

The Physical Abuse index is based on the average of three survey questions.
The range is from 1 (low) to 5 (high)

High scores by parents on this measure of physical abuse correlate with the following characteristics of both child and parent:

youth conflict with authority
coercive parents
nagging parents
negative peer pressure
worry about parent drinking
parent worry about excessive punishment
authoritarian controls
youth fear of sexual aggression
parent-child misunderstanding
youth worry about physical development[8]

High scores on physical abuse by parents are *negatively* associated with measures of

parental nurturance
family closeness
parent age
the self-esteem of both parents

VIOLENCE BETWEEN PARENTS

The concluding topic of this chapter is an examination of parents' reports of conflict in their marriage. This measure of spouse conflict has been used by other researchers in the area of family violence, and the behaviors are listed in the order of increasing violence as reported in an article by M.A. Straus.[9] Parents were asked to respond to the following set of instructions.

No matter how well a couple get along, there are times when they disagree, or get upset with each other. At such times, they use many different methods of trying to settle their differences.
Below is a list of ways your partner may have acted toward you during a disagreement or argument. Think back *over the last twelve months* and make your best estimate of how many times your partner did each of these things. Your response choices are: never; once or twice; 3 to 5 times; 6 to 10 times; 11 times or more.

Here are their responses, listed in the order of reported frequency. Note the similarity of responses by mothers and fathers.

			Percent Reporting	
Spouse Activity	*None*	*1–2 times*	*3–10 times*	*11 or more times*
My partner talked calmly				
Mothers	10	31	40	19
Fathers	6	33	44	17
Raised voice, etc.				
Mothers	31	31	26	12
Fathers	33	34	25	9
Refused to talk				
Mothers	34	36	22	8
Fathers	29	41	24	6
Threw, kicked, or broke things				
Mothers	80	14	4	2
Fathers	82	14	4	1
Pushed, shoved, grabbed me				
Mothers	86	10	2.5	1.5
Fathers	87	10	2	1
Hit, kicked, slapped me				
Mothers	93	4	1.0	1.4
Fathers	91	7	1.4	1.2
Threw things at me				
Mothers	95	3	0.7	1.3
Fathers	92	6	1.3	1.1
Beat me up				
Mothers	98	0.8	0.3	1.1
Fathers	98	0.4	0.5	1.1

The largest difference occurs in the 8 percent of fathers who report that their partner threw things at them, compared to 5 percent of mothers who report similar behavior by their partner. Two percent of both sexes report being beaten by a partner at least once during the past year. These data clearly indicate that serious conflict and violence are regular occurrences in 5 to 10 percent of homes represented in this population and less frequent in many more.

RELATIONSHIP OF SPOUSE VIOLENCE TO OTHER FAMILY CHARACTERISTICS

We grouped all spousal behavior (with the exception of "talking calmly") to form a measure of violence. We then compared this measure with other elements of the study to discover what links it has with other facets of personal or family life.[10]

Not surprisingly, the strongest links were the negative ones. The following are *unlikely* to accompany family life in which spouse violence occurs:

Family harmony (reported by either the child or parents)
High quality of life (reported by parents)
Family closeness (reported by child)

These, on the other hand, often accompany family life in which spouse violence occurs:

Abuse of the child (reported by child and parents)
Coercive methods of discipline (reported by child and parents)
Economic stress (reported by parents)
Dissatisfaction with the family's standard of living (reported by mother)
Alcoholism in the family (reported by mother)
Child in conflict with authority (reported by father)

SUMMARY AND INTERPRETATION

In studying this group of parents and children, we find, as other researchers have found,[11] that parenting styles are closely linked to young adolescents' values and behaviors. These connections are among the strongest in the entire study. In capsule form, these findings are:

Four parenting behaviors—demonstrative affection, nurturance, democratic control, and inductive discipline—are strongly tied to social-emotional health in the young adolescent and correlate *positively* with his or her

self-esteem
social competence
prosocial behavior
achievement motivation
internalization of moral values
concern for people and the world

They are *negatively* related to
social alienation
aggression
standard-breaking behavior
chemical use[12]

Four parenting behaviors—authoritarian control, permissive control, coercive discipline, and love withdrawal—have a negative effect on what young adolescents value and do, and tend to correlate with a number of measures.

Each of these is *positively* associated with
> aggression
> social alienation
> chemical use

They are *negatively* associated with
> self-esteem
> prosocial behavior
> social competence.[13]

Several possible explanations for these findings come to mind. One is this: affection, nurturance, inductive discipline, and democratic control contribute to a family mileau in which young adolescents have both support and freedom within well-explained, even negotiable limits. This combination produces good feelings about oneself, good feelings about one's parents, and internalization of rules and norms parents consider important. On the other hand, authoritarian control, coercive discipline (which correlate highly with each other), love withdrawal, and permissive control do not provide young adolescents with either a sense of caring support or responsible limits, nor do they build a sense of self-confidence or a sense of self-importance. Since authoritarian control is overpunitive, and permissive control is overlenient, both are likely to be applied inconsistently and sporadically. Such lack of predictability prevent the child from learning what the limits are. In addition, authoritarian control and coercive discipline encourage rebellion against parental wishes.

The evidence from this study, as well as from others, strongly suggests these conclusions:

· That affection, nurturance, democratic control, and inductive discipline promote healthy development.
· That authoritarian control, coercive discipline, love withdrawal, and permissive control inhibit healthy development.

Most of the families in this study apparently use healthy parenting styles. Even so, they are not fully content with their parenting skills, as indicated by their responses to these three items.

	Mothers	*Fathers*
To be a good parent is one of the hardest things I do.		
Percent who "agree" or "strongly agree"	86	76
I am not as good a parent as I should be.		
Percent who "agree" or "strongly agree"	47	53
How much do you worry about the job you are doing raising your child?		
Percent who worry "very much" or "quite a bit"	66	60

Most parents know parenting is hard work. They hunger for improved communication with their child and for ways to improve their parenting skills. Even though many of them are relatively effective parents, we also find some families who suffer the pain of extreme pressures, conflict, and physical violence. Undue pressure applied to children is a phenomenon familiar to anyone in the field of education, and its unhappy cousin, child abuse, is also becoming more recognizable. Research cannot by itself solve these serious problems, but it can make visible the kinds of patterns that accompany them in families and enlarge the understanding of those who discover evidence of their presence in the homes of the youth with whom they work.

CHAPTER 16

When Young Adolescents and Their Families Need Help

- About half of all young adolescents would turn first to their parents for help with problems.
- The percentage of young people seeking help from their parents declines from fifth through ninth grade.
- As parents' value as consultants for their children declines, the value of peer friends as consultants increases.
- Parents view members of the clergy as a likely source of help with parenting problems.
- A higher percentage of fathers than mothers prefer to handle problems entirely on their own.
- Understanding sex is one of the few topics in which boys are more interested than girls.
- Parents' priorities for topics on which they might receive help have some surprising similarities to the priorities chosen by their children.
- Almost half of young adolescents would like to talk more with their parents about the topic of right and wrong.
- Girls show more interest in conversation with parents than do boys, and mothers show more interest in conversation with children than do fathers.

When trouble comes, where do young adolescents turn? To whom do they look for help and advice? Whom can they trust to be willing to listen, and to provide wisdom and support when they're in a jam? And where do parents turn for help? Who are the authorities and the care-givers that parents go to when they seek advice or comfort or simply want to do a better job of being parents?

Youth and parent surveys both included questions about the kinds of people from whom they would seek help if they needed it.

YOUNG ADOLESCENTS' CHOICES

We asked young adolescents who they would turn to for help and advice in several situations. Here are the situations, the possible sources of help, and the percentage of young adolescents who would seek help from each source.

Percent who would most likely *seek help from this source*

Problem	Parent	Peer Friend	Adult Friend	Relative	Clergy	Teacher	Nobody
When having trouble in school	51	17	4	5	2	18	3
When wondering how to handle my feelings	48	24	6	7	4	3	9
When my friends start using drugs or alcohol	40	16	9	7	6	11	11
When having questions about sex	50	20	7	8	3	2	11
When feeling guilty about something I did	38	25	6	7	10	3	10
When deciding what to do with my life	63	8	5	5	4	5	10
Average of all six situations	48	18	6	7	5	7	9

Young adolescents view parents as the most likely source of help; about half of these young adolescents would turn to them on every kind of problem mentioned. Peers are the second choice as sources of help.

In all situations except school trouble (a problem that may seem less difficult to admit than the others), about 10 percent of the sample would not turn to anyone—a rather bleak finding. There are some lonely youngsters out there carrying their troubles in silence.

Other parts of this report show that the desire to spend time with parents tends to diminish as students pass upward through the grades. Might we assume, then, that the tendency to depend on parents for help in times of trouble also diminishes through the grades? Our survey explored this question with the following results. (Note that the highest percentage for each question is starred.)

Percent who most likely *would choose parents for help or advice . . .*	5th	6th	7th	8th	9th	Total
When having trouble in school	54	56*	55	48	41	51
When wondering how to handle my feelings	58*	56	47	42	36	48
When some of my friends start using drugs or alcohol	45	46*	41	35	31	40
When having questions about sex	57*	56.5	51	46	38	50
When feeling guilty about something I have done	47*	43	39	34	29	38
When deciding what to do with my life	61	62	64	65*	62	63
Average of all six situations	54*	53	50	45	40	

* = highest-percentage for that problem

These observations are noteworthy:

- In five of the six situations presented, the highest percentage choosing parents as source of help is among fifth and sixth graders.
- In five of the six situations presented, the lowest percentage choosing parents as source of help is in ninth grade.
- When all six situations are taken together, the percentage choosing parents as source of help declines steadily from fifth through ninth grade.
- The one question that does not fit the pattern of the other five is about vocation—"deciding what to do with my life." On this question the percentage turning to parents *rises* from fifth to eighth grade but declines slightly in ninth. Even so, more than 60 percent in all of the grades represented choose parents as resource on this important question.

We find little difference in the willingness of boys and of girls to seek out the various sources of help. Where boys and girls do differ is in their tendency to turn to peer friends as a source of help. The following shows the percentage of boys and girls who would turn to peer friends as they progress through the grades.

Percent who most likely *would turn to peers for help or advice* . . .	5th	6th	7th	8th	9th
When having trouble in school					
Boys	11	12	12	17	22
Girls	11	13	20	26	27
When wondering how to handle my feelings					
Boys	9	12	17	21	22
Girls	14	23	30	39	41
When some of my friends start using drugs or alcohol					
Boys	11	11	14	20	25
Girls	8	12	16	20	25
When having questions about sex					
Boys	16	16	19	22	26
Girls	10	14	20	25	30
When feeling guilty about something I have done					
Boys	15	18	17	24	26
Girls	15	24	32	35	43
When deciding what to do with my life					
Boys	6	9	7	7	8
Girls	7	8	9	9	8
Average of all six situations					
Boys	11	13	14	19	22
Girls	11	16	21	26	29

These observations are noteworthy:

· The percentage choosing peer friends as a source of help rises steadily from fifth through ninth grade almost without exception for both boys and girls. The sole exception to the rising pattern occurs on decisions about the future.
· A greater percentage of girls seeks peer help with emotional problems and with problems of guilt in all the grades, and the percentage of those who do so rises more sharply than does the percentage of boys.
· On decisions about the future, peer friends are chosen by very few as sources of help.
· Even though young adolescents are more likely to seek advice from peers with each succeeding grade and even though the percentage who say they

are likely to seek advice from parents falls, peers' influence, when averaged across all six situations, never rises above 29 percent for girls and 22 percent for boys.

In summary, the lowest average percentage who would seek *parental* help (occuring in ninth grade) is 40 percent. For young adolescents at this age, parents are still the primary providers of comfort, support, and advice. Figure 43 shows a comparison of parents and peers as sources of help.

PARENTS' CHOICES

We offered parents a different set of problems and a different list of possible sources of help. Here are the situations, potential sources of help, and the percentage of mothers and fathers who would seek each source. (Note that highest percentage for each is starred.)

Figure 43   Young Adolescents' Source of Help: Parents or Peers?

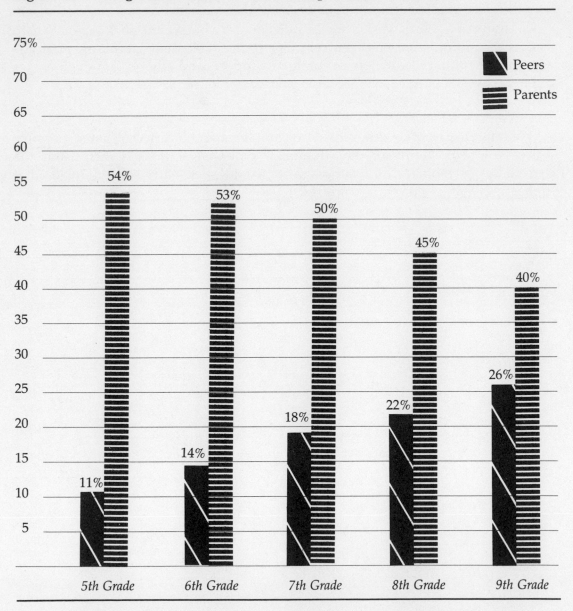

Percents shown are the average of young adolescents choosing parents or peers as source of help in six situations.

Percent who would seek this source of help first

Problem	Nobody	Relative	Friend or Neighbor	Clergy	Medical Doctor	School Official	Community Agency
If my child got involved with drugs or alcohol							
Mother	8	9	4	30*	20	7	22
Father	20	4	4	31*	16	7	18
If my child became depressed and sad for a long time							
Mother	5	6	3	21	44*	11	10
Father	12	4	3	24	37*	11	8
If my child had a lot of questions about sex I couldn't answer							
Mother	14	8	6	10	50*	8	4
Father	18	6	4	17	38*	12	5
If my child was getting into trouble a lot							
Mother	10	6	4	37*	1	29	13
Father	26	4	3	31*	1	23	12
If my child was hanging around too much with kids I did not like							
Mother	49*	6	10	15	0.4	18	2
Father	69*	2	6	11	0.4	11	1

			Percent who would seek this source of help first				
Problem	*Nobody*	*Relative*	*Friend or Neighbor*	*Clergy*	*Medical Doctor*	*School Official*	*Community Agency*
If I needed to know more about how to discipline my child effectively							
Mother	13	11	10	26*	2	20	17
Father	19	9	9	30*	2	18	14
If I (or my husband or wife) had a hard time being kind or loving to my child							
Mother	11	10	6	52*	4	1	15
Father	15	9	5	56*	3	1	10

* = highest percentage choosing this source of help

The following observations are worth noting:

· Clergy are the first choice as source of help on four issues and, overall, are parents' most likely source.
· Physicians are the first choice of parents on two issues—depression and questions related to sex.
· In general, mothers are more willing than fathers to seek help from community professionals—physicians, school personnel, or someone from a community agency.
· Relatives and friends are the resources least likely to be relied on for aid in the named situations.
· More fathers than mothers, on every question presented, would try to handle the question on their own, without consulting anyone.

ORGANIZATIONS AS SOURCES OF HELP

Another way in which we inquired into the kinds of help parents and youth would seek was to list a variety of kinds of learning and to ask whether or not parents and youth would be interested if it were offered in some kind of group setting.

The following includes the list of topics we provided young adolescents, along with their responses.

Topic	Percent much interest	Rank	Percent much interest plus some interest	Rank
Learning how to make friends and be a friend	61	1	93	2
Finding out what is special about me	51	2	92	3
Figuring out what it means to be a Christian	51	3	88	7
Learning about what is right and wrong	50	4	91	4
Talking with other kids about things that are really important	41	5	91	5
Learning how to talk better with adults	40	6	90	6
Learning how to deal with drugs and alcohol	31	7	65	9
Finding out how to do something good for others	31	8	94	1
Understanding sex better	30	9	79	8
Figuring out what it means to be Jewish	10	10	38	10

The testimony of numbers is sometimes ambiguous and requires interpretation. The numbers on these ten topics give us two slightly different messages, depending on how we structure the ranking. The preceding chart shows at left the ranking of the ten topics when only the percentage of those who said they were *much interested* is taken into account. At the right is shown the ranking of the topics when the percentage of those who indicated *much interest* is combined with those who had *some interest*.

Certain things come clear from studying these figures. First, personal identity (finding out what is special about me) and relationship skills (learning how to make friends and be a friend) are at or near the top of both lists. These are two areas where anxieties and interest are high as the period of young adolescence sets in. As the young person's preference for being with family over being with friends gradually diminishes and the importance and power of the peer group rapidly increases, the young person begins to ask questions he or she has not considered before: Now that I'm out here, alone, exposed, no longer comfortable staying in my ready-made family unit, who am I? And these other people with whom I want to be associated, who are they? How do I make contact with them? I wish somebody would tell me how I should go about making friends.

Considered together, the rankings may seem contradictory. In the first ranking, the altruistic topic, "Finding out how to do something good for other people," stands in the eighth-ranked position, drawing much interest from only 31 percent. Teens' highest priorities are elsewhere. Adding the 64 percent who said they had *some interest*, however, propels the topic to the top of the preference list. Despite the probable influence of their surroundings at the time of the survey (church basements, youth rooms), the fact that most youth have at least some interest in learning how to do good things for other people should be taken seriously.

GRADE AND SEX DIFFERENCES

Do the interests of young adolescents vary from grade to grade? Are some educational programs best offered in the fifth or sixth grade and others in the eighth or ninth? How much difference is there between boys' interests and girls' interests in the topics offered?

The following chart (see p. 209) presents the information. The degree of interest girls express in each of the first seven topics is strikingly high when compared with the interest of boys. On "learning how to make friends and be a friend," the level of interest diverges most dramatically in the eighth grade, at which point 72 percent of girls have *much interest* in friendship skills and only 47 percent of boys have such an interest.

Percent much interested *by grade*

		5th	6th	7th	8th	9th
Learning how to make friends and be a friend	Boys	54	56	53	47	52
	Girls	70	67	67	72	71
Finding out what is special about me	Boys	48	49	46	46	43
	Girls	54	53	56	56	60
Learning about what is right and wrong	Boys	55	47	46	44	40
	Girls	60	57	53	49	49
Figuring out what it means to be a Christian	Boys	53	50	49	44	43
	Girls	56	56	52	51	54
Talking with other kids about things that are really important	Boys	38	36	37	35	32
	Girls	42	43	46	49	51
Learning how to talk better with adults	Boys	44	38	40	34	32
	Girls	43	41	44	38	43
Finding out how to do something good for other people	Boys	38	26	27	20	22
	Girls	39	34	33	31	37
Learning how to deal with drugs and alcohol	Boys	31	33	33	30	27
	Girls	30	31	35	29	29
Understanding sex better	Boys	25	32	36	36	36
	Girls	27	26	29	27	31
Figuring out what it means to be Jewish	Boys	18	12	11	8	9
	Girls	14	11	8	7	6

On the topic of "finding out how to do something good for other people," the discovery that stands out is that, whereas boys and girls show nearly identical interest in the topic in fifth grade, girls' interest decreases slightly, grade by grade, through the eighth grade, but boys' interest drops more sharply through the grades until, by ninth grade, boys and girls are fifteen percentage points apart.

On the two communications topics, we see only a slight difference of interest between boys and girls, particularly as regards talking with adults. There is only a slight difference in boys' and girls' interest in holding important conversations with peers in the early grades, but while the boys' interest stays about steady, the girls' interest rises, peaking in the eighth grade.

If programs in these topics draw more girls than boys, these data suggest that no amount of coaxing or welcoming strategies will overcome boys' reluctance. They simply lack interest in such topics. Many boys, at this age, appear to have other priorities.

On the two topics with moral/ethical content the interest of both sexes declines through the grades, but both (except for girls on one question) show a renewed interest in the ninth grade.

PARENTS' INTEREST IN OPPORTUNITIES FOR LEARNING

Near the end of the parent survey, parents were asked about their interest in seven topics for which programs might be designed to help them learn more effective parenting skills. The topic and the percentage of parents "very interested" and "quite interested" in such programs appear here.

A program that helps parents learn:	*Fathers*	*Mothers*
How to help a child develop healthy concepts of right and wrong	65	73
How to help a child grow in religious faith	60	71
More about drugs	63	68
How to have better communication with their children	57	68
Effective discipline	41	52
More about sex education	40	48
How to participate in support groups where parents talk with other parents about common problems of being a parent	34	50

These findings from the data are worth noting:

· Helping children distinguish between right and wrong comes as top priority for parents' learning.
· Parents' second priority is another topic linked with morality—their children's growth in religious faith.

· Parents show considerable interest in most topics listed; in even the lowest-rated topic (support groups), about one third are interested.

One of the much-debated but unanswered questions of the eighties is whether the differences exhibited in the thought and behavior of men and of women are inherent in maleness and femaleness or whether the differences are brought about by the unspoken and unexamined assumptions of the culture that gradually shapes the thought and behavior of both sexes. This study affords some insights into at least a limited portion of this disputed territory. Does, for example, the interest of parents in learning better methods of discipline change depending on the sex of the child? Does a parent exhibit more interest in good communications with a girl than with a boy? Are parents more eager to foster the development of faith in one sex than the other?

We did not find that parents have different degrees of concern about parenting for girls and boys. Topic by topic, the percentage of concern parents express is always within one or two points for boys and for girls. On all seven topics, mothers are far more willing than fathers to seek or to accept help with parenting. The issue on which parents' willingness to be helped is most nearly the same is drug education. The issue on which they are most different is their interest in joining a support group of parents.

Although the list of learning opportunities offered to parents is shorter than the list offered to their children (seven topics rather than ten), the two lists contain four parallels, as illustrated below.

Parent Topic	*Child Topic*
More about sex education	Understanding sex better
More about drugs	Learning how to deal with drugs and alcohol
How to have better communication with their children	Learning how to talk better with adults
How to help a child develop health concepts of right and wrong.	Learning about what is right and wrong

The first question that comes to mind about these four topics is this: Do parents and children share the same interests in learning? The following figure shows the relative interest of mothers, fathers, and youth in the listed topics.

	Youth ("much interest")	Father ("very" and "quite interested")	Mother
Concepts of right and wrong	50	65	73
Youth/adult communication	40	57	67
Drug/alcohol education	31	63	68
Sex education	30	40	49

The figure above shows that

· For each topic, the young people's interest is lowest, the fathers' next, and the mothers' highest.
· Concepts of right and wrong are of greatest interest to both parents and children.
· Of the four, the topic of least concern to both is sex education. This may be at least in part due to the fact that something labeled "sex education" is included in the school curriculum for many students of about this age, and similar courses are available in many locations through other community agencies.
· Youth rank communication with adults next to the top in priority among these parallel four.

PARENT-CHILD COMMUNICATION

We presented youth with a list of things they might want to talk with their parents about. The parent survey contained a similar list.

There is a kind of poignancy about the longings that underlie the data from these lists. We find that young people want to talk to their parents about issues that interest them, puzzle them, trouble them and that parents want to talk with their children. But, in most instances, the conversations never happen.

To be sure, some talking takes place, but only in some families, and, even for them, not often enough, or for long enough. Too often, household routines, school schedules, the family's comings and goings, and television's mesmerizing distractions carry parents and children along, week after week, until suddenly the children are graduating from high school, and all the things they meant some day to talk about—and the right times to do it—have vanished.

The lists were not identical, nor were the possible answers. The nine questions on the youth survey were presented like this:

What things would you like to talk *more* with your parents (or parent) about, and what things would you like to talk *less* with them about? For each of the following, tell if it is something you want to talk about *more*, *less*, or *the same amount* as you do now.

*How I dress and wear my hair
 How my parents and I get along
*Drugs or alcohol
*My friends
*How I'm doing in school
*My ideas of what is right and wrong
*Questions I have about sex
 Problems my parents have
 What my parents expect of me

(*These topics are common to the parents' list.)

We presented eleven questions to parents with these instructions:

Some parents would like a chance to talk more to their children about important topics. Below is a list of topics. For each one, tell if it is something you would like to talk with your child more about: "definitely," "probably," "not sure," "probably not," "definitely not."

*Drugs and alcohol
*My child's questions about sex
*My child's friends
*My child's views of right and wrong
*School
*How my child dresses and wears his or her hair
 God and other religious topics
 World events
 My child's hopes and dreams
 My child's worries and concerns
 My love for my child

(*These topics are common to the child's list.)

Comparison of interest between youth and adults follows.

Topic	Percent less	Percent more
My ideas of what is right and wrong		
Youth	15	47
Mother		43
Father		34
How I'm doing in school		
Youth	18	46
Mother		37
Father		29
My friends		
Youth	16	44
Mother		28
Father		19
Questions I have about sex		
Youth	26	39
Mother		50
Father		33
Drugs or alcohol		
Youth	26	33
Mother		42
Father		38
How I dress and wear my hair		
Youth	22	26
Mother		11
Father		8

These findings, we think, are significant:

· Almost half (46%) of the youth sample would like to talk more with their parents about the topic of right and wrong. Only 15 percent say they'd like less discussion of the topic. Parents—43 percent of mothers and 34 percent of fathers—also express definite interest.
· Conversation about school performance (46%) and friends (44%) are almost as popular with young people as the topic of right and wrong.
· On drugs and alcohol, youth split almost perfectly into thirds: 33 percent want more discussion, 33 percent want less, and the remaining 34 percent are satisfied with the amount of discussion they now have.
· Mothers' top interest in more discussion is the topic of sex (50%), and fathers' top interest in more discussion is the topic of drugs and alcohol (38%).

· In general, younger youth want communication with their parents more than older youth, and girls are slightly more interested in discussion than are boys. (See Figure 44.)

· Mothers express more interest than fathers in more conversation with their child on each of the topics. Mothers and fathers come closest to expressing the same degree of interest on the topics of drugs and the child's appearance.

ASKED OF YOUTH ONLY

The three topics listed on the youth survey but not asked of parents are listed below along with young adolescents' responses.

Topic of Conversation	*Amount of Communication Desired:*		
	Percent less	*Percent same*	*Percent more*
How my parents and I get along	14	37	49
Problems my parents have	24	38	38
What my parents expect of me	18	35	47

· Of these three topics, on only the first—getting along with parents—are there differences among youth related to their sex and grade in school. The percentage of boys wanting more communication with parents declined by 21 percentage points (from 60% to 39%) between fifth and ninth grade, and ten percentage points (from 57% to 47%) for girls.

· Nearly half of all youth want to talk more with their parents about how they get along together (49%) and what parents expect of them (47%).

· Some young adolescents are wary of getting further involved in problems that trouble their parents, with one fourth wanting less of such involvement but a somewhat surprising 38 percent willing to become further involved in discussing adults' problems.

ASKED OF PARENTS ONLY

Topics on the parent survey but not asked of youth are these, along with parent responses:

Figure 44   Index of Youth's Desire for More Communication with Parents

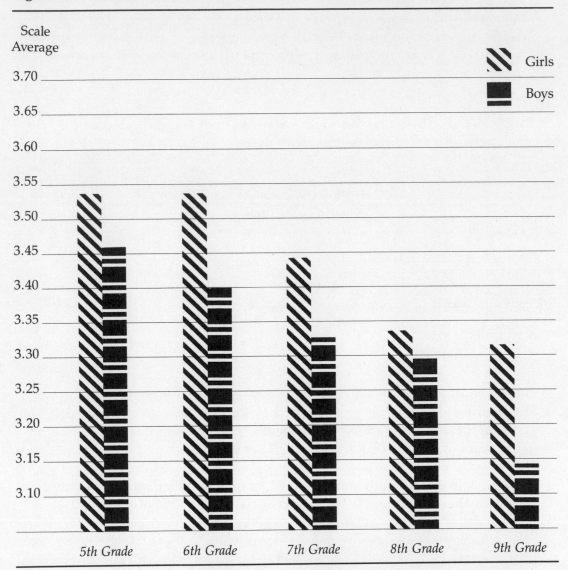

The figures shown are the mean of responses to 5 youth items, with 1 = want to talk less and 5 = want to talk more:

How I dress and wear my hair
How my parents and I get along
My friends

How I'm doing in school
My ideas of what is right and wrong

Topic	*Percent who want more communication*
My child's worries and concerns	
Mother	68
Father	50
My love for my child	
Mother	61
Father	47
My child's hopes and dreams	
Mother	61
Father	44
God and other religious topics	
Mother	40
Father	28
World events	
Mother	14
Father	12

We note that

· Mothers show considerably more interest than fathers in talking with their child on all of these topics except for world events, a topic which apparently interests few parents.

· Two thirds of mothers and half of fathers express definite interest in more talk with their child about her or his worries. This interest may relate to our finding, in Chapter 4, that they are not accurately in touch with the degree and nature of their children's worries. Parents' responses here suggest that they sense that gap of understanding.

· We find no difference between parents of sons and parents of daughters in their desire for parent-child conversation, and no difference according to the child's grade in school.

COMMENT

It is generally recognized that the task of parenting has become more difficult in the Western world in the twentieth century than it once was. Extended families are now the exception rather than the rule; in more families both parents work outside the home; and children and teens today are surrounded by more temptations, distractions, and conflicting forces than were their parents during adolescence.

SOURCES OF HELP

Parents need help with the problems of being a parent; young people need help growing up in this complex society and grappling with its conflicting messages. Evidence from this study seems to indicate that females—both girls and mothers—conclude more readily than males that they need help and are more willing than males to seek that help. Unless substantial shifts of sex-role expectation suddenly occur, those who provide resources for parents can expect to be consulted more often by mothers than by fathers.

Evidence of the gradually diminishing influence of parents as their children progress through the grades appears a number of times in these data. It appears once again in young adolescents' choices of persons to whom they turn for help. Clearly, the prime time for parents to establish a warm and open relationship with their children is throughout the elementary grades, if not before. Happily, many parents in this study appear to have successfully established that relationship, since, even in ninth grade, from about one third to two thirds of youth would still take their problems first to their parents.

GROUP LEARNING FOR YOUTH

Offering opportunities for learning is a major way in which organized groups—community agencies, educational organizations, churches—serve the needs of youth. The priorities expressed by so large a group of youngsters, assessed nationwide, are an important guide to the areas in which the young people themselves feel a need.

The high ranking of "learning how to make friends and be a friend" should be no surprise to anyone who knows this age well. Youth programming has neglected practical, "how-to" help in this area, believing that simply bringing groups of youngsters together in the context of a game or activity will somehow result in friendships. For the more socially skillful teenager, this probably is enough. But substantial numbers of young people are hungry for ways to learn practical social skills—ways of talking, listening, relating—that help make friends more efficiently than the trial and error methods they've been using. Often enough, these trial and error methods result in embarrassment or pain, and the young person grows wary. Youth programming can provide resources to help youngsters learn the skill of making friends.

The relatively low evidence of interest in learning more about drug abuse and human sexuality, expressed particularly by fifth and sixth graders, as compared with interest expressed in other areas, deserves careful interpretation. Some things that are essential for the care and nurture of elementary school students do not necessarily come at the top of their personal priority lists. Evidence from other parts of the survey suggests that at least some fifth and sixth graders could profit from study of human sexuality. Some fifth and sixth graders who claimed that they had engaged in sexual intercourse may not have accurately understood what the term meant. Even so, 39 percent of fifth graders and 47 percent of sixth graders said that they "are in love with someone my age of the opposite sex," and if these figures are accurate (we have no reason to doubt them), they reinforce the belief of many observers that experiences and knowledge of what were once thought to be adult matters occur earlier in present-day youth. Clearly, then, education in human sexuality cannot wait until these young adolescents are in high school. Some form of instruction about sex may be appropriate in the upper elementary grades. Certainly, one might wish that the 17 percent of eighth graders and the 20 percent of ninth graders who said they had engaged in intercourse had been introduced, at an earlier age, to the pitfalls and responsibilities attached to physical intimacy.

Chemical abuse, too, appears to occur at an ever earlier age. Consequently, our young people need to know more than they may think or want about drug abuse and the attitudes, feelings, and circumstances that accompany it.

GROUP LEARNING FOR PARENTS

One of several pieces of good news in this chapter comes in the number of parents who are seeking opportunities to learn better parenting skills.

Another piece of hopeful news is that parents and youth share similar interests and concerns. Both children and adults would like to find greater clarity on moral issues and ways to work together on developing guidelines for behavior.

A third piece of good news is that youth rank communication with adults as high as they do. This, together with the evidence earlier in the chapter that parents are the most likely resource when young adolescents are in trouble, should provide strong support to parents' sense of their own value to their children.

COMMUNICATION IN THE FAMILY

Some may be surprised that so many young people would like *more* discussion with their parents about the topic of right and wrong. Much of the day-to-day material of parent-child controversy no doubt centers on that topic already, and no doubt parent and child often approach it from opposite directions. But these conversations tend to center on specific and immediate situations in which each has certain conflicting and perhaps unspoken investments. One example is the frequent disagreement over curfew. Perhaps more discussion of right and wrong attracts young adolescents because they hope that through a better understanding of one another's general points of view on moral questions they may be able to find some common ground from which they can work toward greater family harmony.

Our survey results clearly demonstrate that youth and parents alike want to talk more to each other. We believe there are at least four reasons why they do not. First, most parents and children lack the *skills* needed to communicate on topics important to them both without hurting each other. Second, they lack the kind of *at-home diplomacy* that is similar to but not exactly like the diplomacy of any other social unit. Third, they lack an appropriate *trigger event*, some person or event that raises the subject for conversation at a time when neither has an immediate investment in the conversation's coming out a particular way (for example, an occasion to discuss appropriate weekday and weekend curfew hours when the question of why the teenager came home so late last night is not under discussion).

Finally, and perfectly understandably, they lack the *courage* to take on an issue. Talking about moral issues that have implications for their daily life together takes emotional energy. Everyone who enters the discussion runs the risk of hurt—of hearing things they would rather not hear, of discovering circumstances that may come as an unpleasant surprise. Conversations on topics that touch vulnerable points are conversations that most people would *like to have had*. To emerge on the other side of such a discussion whole, with ego not severely bruised and with greater understanding, would be a considerable triumph. But the fear of risks ahead looms large when one decides, finally, "I'll take the bull by the horns, and we'll talk."

Agencies that work with youth and families can be of great help with all four ingredients necessary to positive family communication: skill, home diplomacy, trigger event, and courage. Programs that teach communication skills and the style of diplomacy appropriate to the family setting are available and can be taught. Such programs offered to parents and youth can provide the trigger event for the conversation to take place. And the leader or teacher of such groups can offer support that encourages both parents and children to learn these important conversational skills, to try them out safely, and then to use them at home.

Scarcely any gift would contribute more to the total welfare of parents and their children than the opportunity to learn when and how to say to each other the things that both are longing to say.

Appendix

METHODOLOGICAL NOTES

The research project "Young Adolescents and Their Parents" began in 1980, under a major grant from The Lilly Endowment, Inc. The project brought together the research capability of Search Institute and the programming expertise of thirteen national youth-serving organizations. The research component included a 319-item survey given to 8,165 young people in grades five through nine, and to 10,467 of their parents.

SAMPLING

For most of the thirteen national agencies, a two-stage sampling procedure was used. In the first stage, the selection of local units was stratified by geography and local unit size (in most cases, congregation size). In the second stage, young adolescents in each local unit were randomly selected from a master list of all fifth through ninth graders affiliated with the local unit. These lists included both active and inactive youth. Sampling ratios were used to ensure that, for each of the thirteen national organizations, every young adolescent affiliated with that organization had an equal possibility of being selected.

ENLISTMENT

Once samples of local units were drawn, each of the thirteen national organizations sought to enlist the cooperation of its sample of local units. A combination of letters from national headquarters and phone follow-ups was used. Noncooperating local units were not replaced. Enlistment occurred in the spring and summer of 1982. Depending on the size of the local unit, either all or a random sample of young adolescents were selected for participation. In addition, the parents of each invited young adolescent were asked to respond to the parent survey.

ADMINISTRATION

In each local unit, a project coordinator was designated. All project coordinators received identical administration manuals. These manuals standardized the process for randomly selecting young adolescents, enlisting the cooperation of selected young adolescents, enlisting the cooperation of young adolescents' parents, and administering the surveys. In most local units, young adolescents and parents assembled in one room to hear overall instructions and to receive survey forms and answer sheets. Youth and parents then proceeded to different rooms to take the survey. Average administration time for young adolescents was one hour and forty-five minutes, and for parents, one and one-half hours. A survey number process made it possible to later match the answer sheets of youth and their parent(s) for purposes of analysis.

To protect confidentiality, a number of steps were taken. No lists matching names and answer sheet numbers were created. Answer sheets did not ask for a respondent's name or city. Upon completion of the survey, each respondent placed the survey form in a large envelope at the front of the room. When all survey forms were placed in the envelope, it was sealed and mailed. Respondents were assured that answer sheets could not be returned to local units and that all reports would be in aggregate form.

COOPERATION RATES

Of the 1513 local units (clubs, congregations, schools, and residential facilities) drawn into the thirteen national samples, 953 participated, for a 63 percent return rate. No systematic bias in geography, community size, or local unit size was detected in comparing cooperating versus noncooperating local units. Across the 953 units, about 60 percent of the young adolescents drawn in the local unit random samples completed the survey instrument. Ninety percent of the surveys were administered in the fall of 1982, and the remaining 10 percent between January and July 1983.

SURVEY DEVELOPMENT

Survey development proceeded through these steps:

1. In 1980, conceptual frameworks for the content of the youth and parent surveys were established, based on a combination of systematic literature review and the information needs of the thirteen cooperating agencies.
2. In the spring of 1981, 510 young adolescents completed an eight-page list of sentence completion items.
3. In the summer of 1981, first draft instruments were created.

4. In September 1981, instruments were tested, using one hundred low-income fifth and sixth graders, for length, style, comprehension, and wording.
5. In October and November 1981, the instruments were critically reviewed by a team of five social scientists, five junior high school teachers, and seven practitioners (school counselors, clinicians, etc.).
6. Revised instruments were field tested in March 1981, using convenience samples in ten cities. About a thousand young adolescents and four hundred parents participated. Scale reliabilities were computed, and some scales were refined based on this information.

The survey instruments covered a wide range of topics. A list of the topics included in the young adolescent survey follows:

Demographics
Social Context
       Schools
       Friends and Peers
       Church
       Family Characteristics
       Family Dynamics
       Youth Group Involvement
       Mass Media Exposure
       Socioeconomic Indicators
Developmental Processes
       Autonomy
       Maturation and Sexuality
       Identity
       Intimacy
       Achievement
       Social Integration
Beliefs, Attitudes, and Values
       Social Attitudes
       Worries
       Moral Values
       Values
       Religion
Perspectives on Receiving Help
       Sources of Advice and Help
       Desired Programs from Youth Organizations
       Desired Communications with Parents

Behavior

      Prosocial Behavior

      Antisocial Behavior

      Alcohol and Drugs

      Dating and Sexuality

The parent survey covered similar territory, with an additional focus on parenting issues.

SCALES

All scales used in the survey instruments were developed for this project, except for the following:

- The self-esteem measure in the youth survey is based on M. Rosenberg, *Society and the Adolescent Image* (Princeton: N.J.: Princeton University Press, 1965).
- The sex-role orientation scales in the youth survey are based on measures developed by J. A. Hall and Halberstadt, "Masculinity and Femininity in Children: Development of the Children's Personal Attitudes Questionnaire," *Developmental Psychology* 16 (1980), pp 270–280.
- The PAQ was used to measure parent sex-role orientations. See J. J. Spence and R. Helmreich, *Masculinity and Femininity: Their Psychological Dimensions, Correlates, and Antecedents* (Austin: University of Texas Press, 1978).
- The spouse violence scale is based on M.A. Straus, "Leveling, Civility, and Violence in the Family," *Journal of Marriage and the Family* 36 (1974), pp. 13-30.

RELIABILITIES

A document listing items and reliabilities for all scales used in this project is available from Search Institute. Two thirds of the scales in the youth survey have reliabilities in the .60 to .85 range. Most of the remaining third are in the .50 to .60 range. Reliabilities are much stronger for ninth graders than fifth graders. Since the correlations cited in this book were computed on the total young adolescent sample, some correlations may have been underestimated due to weak reliabilities for fifth graders, and perhaps also for sixth graders, though this has not yet been examined.

VALIDITY

There is some evidence available regarding validity of scales. In many areas, mothers and fathers corroborate the self-reports of their children. That is, many youth scales are correlated with parallel parent scales (e.g., perception of family closeness, types of discipline and control). And youth self-reports of behavior are correlated with parents' ratings of their young adolescents' behavior. Additionally, many constructs are related to other constructs as predicted by theory (for example, reported negative peer pressure is tied to antisocial behavior, as are a number of other factors suggested by the work of Richard Jessor; discipline styles are linked to prosocial behavior in ways consistent with Martin Hoffman's theory; how parents exercise control is tied to social competence in a manner consistent with the predictions of Diana Baumrind).

ANALYSES

Grade and sex effects reported in Chapters 2 through 11 were based on two-way analyses of variance, using grade and sex as factors. Except in a few isolated cases, a probability level of .0001 was used as the criterion for significance. Because of the large sample sizes, this level was chosen to minimize reporting differences that had relatively little practical significance.

GROUP COMPARISONS

By agreement with each of the thirteen cooperating agencies, no reports or publications compare data from two or more of these agencies. Each of the thirteen agencies holds sole right to disseminate its data.

Notes

CHAPTER 1

1. J. Lipsitz, *Growing up Forgotten* (Lexington, Mass.: D. C. Heath, 1977), p. 29.
2. J. Kagan, in J. Kagan, and R. Coles, eds., *12 to 16: Early Adolescence* (New York: North, 1972, p. vii.
3. P. L. Benson, P. K. Wood, A. L. Johnson, C. H. Eklin, and J. E. Mills, *1983 Minnesota Survey on Drug Use and Drug-Related Attitudes* (Minneapolis: Search Institute, 1983).
4. *Religion in America*, (Princeton Religious Research Center, 1982), p. 22.
5. National figures are based on 1980 census data.
6. The states in these four census regions are as follows:
   North East: Connecticut, Massachusetts, Maine, New Hampshire, Rhode Island, Vermont, New Jersey, New York, Pennsylvania
   North Central: Illinois, Indiana, Michigan, Ohio, Wisconsin, Iowa, Kansas, Minnesota, Missouri, Nebraska, North Dakota, South Dakota
   South: District of Columbia, Delaware, Florida, Georgia, Virginia, West Virginia, South Carolina, North Carolina, Maryland, Alabama, Kentucky, Mississippi, Tennessee, Arkansas, Louisiana, Oklahoma, Texas
   West: Arizona, Colorado, Idaho, Nevada, New Mexico, Montana, Utah, Wyoming, Alaska, California, Hawaii, Oregon, Washington.
7. Young adolescent family income data is from mothers' survey.
8. National figures based on census figures for ten- to fourteen-year-olds.
9. National figures sum to 94 percent. The Census Bureau reports the other 6 percent as "other urban" and does not indicate how these are distributed by size.
10. Young adolescent data provided by mothers. A mother was designated in the labor force if she reported eleven hours or more per week of a "paid job."
11. National figures based on all women and all men over age twenty-five. It is likely that actual percentages of parents in thirty to forty age range are higher.

CHAPTER 2

NOTE: All reported correlations and F ratios are significant at the .0001 level, unless otherwise noted.
1. For a discussion of research findings related to school transition, see D. A. Blyth, R. G. Simmons, and D. Bush, "The Transition into Early Adolescence: A Longitudinal Comparison of Youth in Two Educational Contexts," *Sociology of Education* 51 (1978), pp. 149–62.
2. Interest in school and these other variables are calculated as follows:

Achievement motivation, $r = .32$
Self-esteem, $r = .26$
Youth-parent conflict, $r = -.23$
School climate, $r = .28$
Drug and alcohol use, $r = -.22$
Antisocial behavior $r = -.25$

3. F grade $= 300.1$ ($p <.0001$); F sex $= .2$ (NS). Post hoc comparisons show a significant decrease in school climate with each increment in grade.
4. Parochial vs. public enrollment and school climate, $r = .15$ ($p <.0001$); school climate and antisocial behavior, $r = -.29$ ($p <.0001$); school climate and drug and alcohol use, $r = -.29$ ($p <.0001$).
5. F sex for rock music $= 7.1$ ($p <.008$). F sex for videogames $= 469$ ($p <.0001$).
6. See, for example, A. H. Stein, and L. K. Friedrich, "The Impact of Television on Children and Youth," in E. Hetherington, ed., *Review of Child Development Research*, vol. 5 (Chicago: University of Chicago Press, 1975).
7. Videogame playing and aggression, $r = .30$ ($p <.0001$).
8. See, for example, W. Simon, and J. Gagnon, "On Psychosexual Development," in D. Goslin, ed., *Handbook of Socialization Theory and Research* (Chicago: Rand McNally, 1969).
9. J. P. Hill, *Understanding Early Adolescence: A Framework* (Carboro, N.C.: Center for Early Adolescence, 1980), p. 9
10. See H. Nelsen, R. Potvin, and J. Shields, *The Religion of Children* (Washington, D.C.: Boys Town Center, Catholic University of America, 1977), for one of the few attempts to explore the religious dimension.
11. The correlations with attitudes toward the church (3-item scale) are as follows:
Religious emphasis in the home, $r = .48$
Mother's importance of religion, $r = .40$
Father's importance of religion, $r = .37$
12. The correlations with the prochurch index (a 6-item scale that combines attitudes toward the church and church participation rates) are as follows:
Concern for people, $r = .31$
Prosocial behavior, $r = .26$
Drug and alcohol use index, $r = -.24$
Antisocial behavior index, $r = -.22$
13. F sex for race segregation (Item 319) is 92.6. Girls are higher than boys at each of the five grade levels.
14. J. Krosnick and C. Judd, "Transitions in Social Influence at Adolescence: Who Induces Cigarette Smoking? "*Developmental Psychology* 18 (1982), pp. 359-68.
15. An overall index of peer influence was computed based on the combination of eight survey items.

	5th	6th	7th	8th	9th
Boys' average on peer influence scale	.347	.395	.434	.524	.585
Girls' average on peer influence scale	.338	.455	.569	.671	.736

F grade $= 159.7$, F sex $= 122.4$, F sex $\times$ grade $= 11.9$
16. F grade for peer pressure to deviance is 33.9; F sex is 336.6
17. See *The Journal of Early Adolescence* (Spring/Summer 1983), for a series of related articles. Note especially the papers by Hershel Thornburg on educational systems, and D. Blyth, R. Simmons, and S. Carlton-Ford on school transitions.

CHAPTER 3

NOTE: All reported correlations and F ratios are significant at the .0001 level unless otherwise noted.
1. J. Lipsitz, *Growing up Forgotten* (Lexington, Mass.: D.C. Heath, 1977).

2. For a review, see D. Keating, "Thinking Processes in Adolescence," in J. Adelson, ed., *Handbook of Adolescent Psychology* (New York: John Wiley & Sons, 1980).

3. These five points are made by Keating (see note 2), as summarized by G. Adams and T. Gullota, *Adolescent Life Experiences* (Monterey, Calif.: Brooks/Cole, 1983).

4. D. Elkind, *The Child and Society* (New York: Oxford University Press, 1979).

5. J. Hill, *Understanding Early Adolescence: A Framework* (Carboro, N.C.: Center for Early Adolescence, 1980). Hill draws an important distinction between emotional independence and behavioral independence.

6. Means for each grade on "to make my own decisions" are as follows:

	5th	6th	7th	8th	9th
	3.20	3.37	3.54	3.66	3.70

F grade is 60.4, with significant differences between each pair of grades except eighth and ninth.

7. F grade for attainment of autonomy (mother's view) is 32.2. For father, F grade is 18.3.

8. F grade for youth-parent conflict is 21.69.

9. For example, 80 percent of mothers and fathers in this survey report that their child "respects my values" (parent item 63).

10. For example, the percentage of mothers who claim that their child is rebellious is 14 percent (based on parent item 60, combining "very much" and "somewhat" categories).

11. F grade for social alienation is 8.4, with the decrease in alienation occurring between fifth and sixth grade. F sex is 19.7.

12. Correlations between social alienation and these variables are as follows:
    self-esteem −.45
    Peer pressure to deviance .31
    Antisocial behavior .21
    Worry about killing self (item 194) .29

13. For a similar argument, see J. Hill, *Understanding Early Adolescence: A Framework*, p. 31.

14. Correlations between social alienation and these variables are as follows:
    Nurturance by mother −.31
    Nurturance by father −.27
    Authoritarian control by mother .28
    Authoritarian control by father .25
    Coercive punishment by mother .24
    Coercive punishment by father .22
    Family closeness −.23

15. For a review of the literature, see E. E. Maccoby and C. N. Jacklin, *The Psychology of Sex Differences* (Stanford, Calif.: Stanford University Press, 1974), and Carol Gilligan, *In a Different Voice* (Cambridge, Mass.: Harvard University Press, 1982).

16. F grade for item 147 is 7.6. F sex is 39.4.

17. F grade for item 66 is 18.6. F sex is 48.5.

18. For item 232, F grade $= 60.88$. F sex $= 177.5$.

19. R. G. Simmons, F. Rosenberg, and M. Rosenberg, "Disturbances in the Self-Image of Adolescence," *American Sociological Review* 38 (1973), pp. 553–68.

20. F sex for self-esteem is 61.1.

21. C. Gilligan, *In a Different Voice* (Cambridge: Harvard University Press, 1982).

22. For feminine sex-roles, F grade $= 10.8$. F sex $= 774$ and F grade $\times$ sex $= 7.3$. For masculine sex-roles, F grade $= 22.5$, and F sex $= 103.3$.

23. Individuals were classified as falling above or below the median (both sexes combined) on the feminine and masculine sex-role scales, and then were sorted into one of four combinations.

24. J. T. Spence, and R. L. Helmreich, *Masculinity and Femininity: Their Psychological Dimensions, Correlates, and Antecedents* (Austin: University of Texas Press, 1978). For a recent critique of the androgyny literature, see M. Taylor and J. Hall, "Psychological Androgyny: Theories, Methods, and Conclusions," *Psychological Bulletin* 92 (1978), pp. 347–66.

25. For parent achievement pressure, F grade $= 16.2$, and F sex $= 81.8$.
26. For achievement motivation, F sex $= 94.3$ and F grade $= 4.8$ ($p < .0008$).
27. For educational aspiration, F grade $= 7.2$ and F sex $= 106.8$.
28. For a review of pubertal changes, see A. Petersen and B. Taylor, "The Biological Approach to Adolescence: Biological Change and Psychological Adaptation," in J. Adelson, ed., *Handbook of Adolescent Development* (New York: Wiley, 1980).
29. F grade for attitude toward premarital sex $= 16.0$. F sex $= 519$.
30. Other studies have also shown a higher intercourse rate for younger subjects. For example, Vener and Stewart report a higher rate for youth thirteen and younger than for youth who are fourteen. See note 31 for reference.
31. A. Vener and C. Stewart, "Adolescent Sexual Behavior in Middle America Revisited: 1970–1973," *Journal of Marriage and the Family* 36 (1974), pp. 728–35.
32. For a review of the literature, see C. Chilman, *Adolescent Sexuality in a Changing American Society* (Washington, D.C.: U.S. Department of HEW, NIH publication 80-1426, 1980), p. 98.
33. Correlation of sexual intercourse with drug and alcohol use index is .50, with antisocial behavior .41.

CHAPTER 4

1. The rank order of the worry items remains the same when ranked by item means.
2. F ratios for grade and sex effects are as follows. All F's are significant at the .0001 level unless otherwise indicated.

	Grade	Sex
193. About how my friends treat me	5.0, $p < .0005$	29.9
194. That I might kill myself	12.0	23.7
195. That I might not be able to get a good job when I'm older	N.S.	15.1
196. That someone might force me to do sexual things I don't want to do	8.5	301.7
197. About how well other kids like me	4.2, $p < .002$	104.9
198. That I might lose my best friend	7.3	88.2
199. That one of my parents will hit me so hard that I will be badly hurt	32.1	49.8
200. That I may die soon	15.9	N.S.
201. that a nuclear bomb might be dropped on America	8.9	53.8
202. About all the drugs and drinking I see around me	N.S.	19.5
203. That one of my parents might die	4.2, $p < .002$	16.1
204. About all the people who are hungry and poor in our country	35.1	29.3
205. That I might get beat up at school	29.9	174.9
206. About whether my body is developing (growing) in a normal way	15.6	N.S.
207. About how much my mother or father drinks	34.0	53.4
208. About how I'm doing in school	N.S.	41.0
209. About my looks	48.7	314.9

	Grade	Sex
210. That my friends will get me in trouble	22.9	37.1
211. About all the violence that happens in our country	10.1	N.S.
212. That my parents might get a divorce	27.5	N.S.

3. W. Beardslee and J. Mack, "The Impact of Nuclear Developments on Children and Adolescents," in *American Psychiatric Association Task Report #20, Psychosocial Aspects of Nuclear Developments* (Washington, D.C.: American Psychiatric Association, 1982).
4. "Growing Reports May Indicate Growing Problem," 1984, January 1, *Minneapolis Star and Tribune*.

CHAPTER 5

NOTE: All reported correlations and F ratios are significant at the .0001 level.
1. E. Staub, *Positive Social Behavior and Morality: Social and Personal Influences* (New York: Academic Press, 1978).
2. L. Kohlberg, *Essays in Moral Development* (New York: Harper & Row, 1981).
3. Correlations are as follows:
      Lying with norm-breaking scale, $r = .30$
      Shoplifting with norm-breaking scale, $r = .24$
      Drinking with alcohol use scale, $r = .41$

CHAPTER 6

NOTE: All reported correlations and F ratios are significant at the .0001 level, unless otherwise indicated.
1. For example, the correlation between mothers' attribution to young adolescents of concern for the poor and young adolescents' value on "to have a world without hunger or poverty" is .14. Similar relationships exist on the dimensions of being helpful, autonomy, and hedonism. There are no cases in which predicted correspondence of parent and child views did not correlate.
2. For all value items in Table 6.2 showing change between fifth and ninth grade, there is a significant grade effect based on a two-way analysis of variance with grade and sex as independent variables ($p < .0001$ except for items 161 and 162, $p < .001$).
3. These nine value orientations were identified prior to development of the survey instrument. An empirical search for the structure of the twenty-four value items had not been completed by the writing of this report.
4. These summary conclusions are based on an examination of grade effects from two-way analyses of variance. For seven of the nine orientations, the proposed pattern is based on grade effects for the single items used to define the orientation. For two orientations, analyses of variance were computed on scales. For a three-item index of hedonism, F grade $= 3.98$ (nonsignificant). For a three-item index of concern for people and the world, F grade $= 8.85$.
5. All noted sex differences are significant at the .0001 level, except for "get a good job" and "look good to other kids," which are significant at the .001 level (based on two-way analyses of variance).
6. F sex for hedonistic scale is 40.1. F sex for the concern for people and the world scale is 81.2.
7. R. Carlson, "Sex Differences in Ego Functioning," *Journal of Consulting and Clinical Psychology, 37*

(1971), pp. 267–77; A. Algren, and D. W. Johnson, "Sex Differences in Cooperative and Competitive Attitudes from the 2nd Through the 12th Grades," *Developmental Psychology* 15 (1979), pp. 45–49.

8. The hedonism and mass media exposure scales are correlated .23. The concern for people and the world and prochurch scales are correlated .30.

CHAPTER 7

NOTE: All reported correlations and F ratios are significant at the .0001 level.

1. F grade = 12.8; F sex = 34.4.
2. F sex = 778.2.
3. Correlations are as follows:
      Racial prejudice and sexism, r = .30
      Youth's racial prejudice and
         mother's racial prejudice, r = .26
      Youth's racial prejudice and
         father's racial prejudice, r = .21
      Youth's sexism and
         mother's sexism, r = .21
      Youth's sexism and
         father's sexism, r = .14
      Youth's racial prejudice and
         mother's authoritarian control
         (youth view) r = .16
      Youth's racial prejudice and
         father's authoritarian control
         (youth view) r = .14
      Youth's sexism and
         mother's authoritarian control, r = .12.
4. For a review of the literature on political socialization, see J. Gallatin, "Political Thinking in Adolescence," in J. Adelson, ed., *Handbook of Adolescent Psychology* (New York: John Wiley, 1980).

CHAPTER 8

NOTE: All reported correlations and F ratios are significant at the .0001 level, unless otherwise indicated.

1. *Religion in America: 1979–1980*, The Princeton Religious Research Center, 1980.
2. Ibid., p. 67.
3. *Religion in America*, The Princeton Religious Research Center, 1982, p. 50.
4. Ibid., p. 50.
5. Three important books that look at youth and religion are: M. P. Strommen, *Research on Religious Development* (New York: Hawthorn Books, 1974); M. P. Strommen, *Five Cries of Youth* (New York: Harper & Row, 1971); and R. H. Potivin, D.R. Hoge, and H. M. Nelson, *Religion and American Youth* (Washington, D.C.: Boys Town Center, 1976).
6. F grade for religious centrality is 4.4 (p <.001); F sex is 41.7; F grade × sex is 5.29 (p <.0003).
7. K. S. Kantzer, "The Charismatics Among Us," *Christianity Today*, 1980, February 22.
8. *Emerging Trends*, May 1980, p. 3.
9. For elaboration on this point, see these two references: R. Goldman, *Religious Thinking from Childhood to Adolescence* (New York: Seabury Press, 1964); D. R. Hoge and G. H. Petrillo, "Development of

Religious Thinking in Adolescence: A Test of Goldman's Theories," *Journal for the Scientific Study of Religion* 17 (1978), pp. 139–54.
10. P. L. Benson and D. L. Williams, *Religion on Capitol Hill: Myths and Realities* (New York: Oxford University Press, 1986).
11. F sex = 68.3; F grade × sex = 4.95.
12. F sex for a horizontal religion scale is 49.3.
13. All correlations cited in the three lists are significant at the .0001 level.
14. Correlation between restricting religion and antisocial behavior is .10; with alcohol use r = .15.
15. Correlation with racial prejudice is .15; with sexism r = .18.
16. The correlation between restricting religion and coercive discipline by mother is .13.

CHAPTER 9

NOTE: All reported correlations and F ratios are significant at the .0001 level, unless otherwise noted.
1. The correlation of the prosocial behavior scale and mother's rating of helpfulness is .18. Wtih the value on giving help, r = .31. With an index of concern for people, r = .34.
2. F sex = 382.0; F grade × sex = 5.1 ($p < .0004$).
3. The findings reported here are consistent with those reported by Martin Hoffman. For a recent review, see M. Hoffman in J. Adelson, ed., *Handbook of Adolescent Psychology* (New York: John Wiley, 1980).

CHAPTER 10

NOTE: All reported correlations and F ratios are significant at the .0001 level.
1. F sex = 511.1.
2. F grade = 63.0; F sex = 66.1.
3. M. Gold and R. J. Petronio, "Delinquent Behavior in Adolescence," in J. Adelson, ed., *Handbook of Adolescent Psychology* (New York: John Wiley, 1980).
4. Correlations are as follows:

	Aggression	*Norm-Breaking*
Peer pressure to deviance	.30	.32
Youth-parent conflict	.27	.32
School climate	−.22	−.30
School interest	−.20	−.23
Media influence	.31	.27

CHAPTER 11

1. H. Zimilies, "The Changing American Child: The Perspective of Educators," *A Report to the National Commission on Excellence in Education*, 1982, p. 8.
2. Ibid., p. 41.
3. L. Johnston et al. *Student Drug Use in America 1975–1982* (Rockville, MD.: National Institute on Drug Abuse, 1982), p. 372.
4. The percentage of national twelve- to thirteen-year-olds and fourteen- to fifteen-year-olds who have used marijuana once or more "in the past year" are 6 percent and 18 percent, respectively. See

National Survey on Drug Abuse, Main Findings (Rockville, MD.: National Institute on Drug Abuse, 1982). The figures in the present study for these two age groups are 12 percent (12-13-year-olds) and 20 percent (14-15-year-olds). The figures are also comparable for alcohol use, once or more ("last twelve months").

5. Correlations for these variables with an Index of Drug and Alcohol Use range from .19 to .31.
6. This finding replicates those of S. R. Burkett and M. White, *Journal for the Scientific Study of Religion* (1974), pp. 455–62.
7. P. L. Benson, A. L. Johnson, C. H. Eklin, J. E. Mills, *Minnesota Survey on Drug Use and Drug-Related Attitudes* (Minneapolis: Search Institute, 1983), p. 100.

CHAPTER 12

1. This analysis is based on parent responses to items 63–70, with response choices of "never true," "seldom true," "sometimes true," "often true," and "very often true" and items 46–61, with a format allowing five choices along a continuum. The extremes of the continua are identified by such words as "shy-outgoing," "sad-happy," "mature-immature," "never gets into trouble-often gets into trouble." Parents were asked to indicate whether their child was "very much like," "somewhat like," or "in the middle" for each continuum.

CHAPTER 14

1. Parent intercorrelations were:
   Political orientation
       (liberal-conservative), $r = .294$
   Hunger and poverty, $r = .326$
   Nuclear weapons, $r = .295$
   Youth correlations with parents:

	Mothers	Fathers
Hunger and poverty, $r =$	.118	.111
Nuclear weapons, $r =$	.121	.112

As above, all of these linear correlations underrepresent the strength of the relationship.
2. Correlations between youth and their parents on the scale measuring racial prejudice are .255 with mothers and .206 with fathers.
3. Correlation of sexist views of mother and child is $r = .203$.
4. Correlations of sexist views with racial prejudice are: .257 for mothers and .324 for fathers. Other correlations are:

	Mothers	Fathers
Horizontal religion, $r =$	−.284	−.194
Restricting religion, $r =$	.184	.181
Mother's educational level, $r =$	−.228	−.170
Importance of religion, $r =$	.201	.202

5. Correlations between sexual permissiveness and selected religious measures for each parent sample are:

	Mothers	Fathers
Value-God at center of my life, $r =$	−.352	−.415
Importance of religion to parent, $r =$	−.332	−.393
Prochurch index—parent, $r =$	−.281	−.367
Attend church—parent, $r =$	−.247	−.309
Youth Religion Measures		
Religious emphasis in the home, $r =$	−.227	−.285
Prochurch index, $r =$	−.189	−.199
Attend church, $r =$	−150	−.173
6. Correlates with liberal political views, $r =$	.185	.195
equality in sex roles, $r =$	.150	.205

7. See D. Byrne, *The Attraction Paradigm* (New York: Academic Press, 1971).
8. All of the questions required to make up the scales reported were asked of both parents and children in the survey, even though space considerations prevent the discussion of many of the parent results here.
9. For similar findings, see D. Hoge, "Transmission of Religious and Social Values from Parents to Teenage Children," *Journal of Marriage and the Family* 44 (1982), pp. 569–80.

CHAPTER 15

NOTE: All reported correlations and F ratios are signifcant at the .0001 level unless otherwise indicated.
1. For affection from father, F grade = 54.3; F sex = 10.06 ($p < .001$). For affection from mother, F grade = 95.0; F sex = 42.3.
2. For mother nurturance, F grade = 11.18; F sex = 25.52. For father nurturance, F grade = 11.97, F sex = 10.95 ($p < .0009$).
3. The conceptualization of these three control styles is based on the work of Diana Baumrind. See, for example, "Early Socialization and Adolescent Competence," in S. E. Dragastin and G. H. Elder, Jr., *Adolescence in the Life Cycle* (Washington, D.C.: Hemisphere Publishing Corporation, 1975).
4. Intercorrelations among measures are in the .17–.30 range.
5. The definitions of these three discipline techniques are based on the work of Martin Hoffman. See, for example, "Moral Internalization, Parental Power, and the Nature of Parent-Child Interaction," *Developmental Psychology* 11 (1975), pp. 228–39.
6. F grade for mothers' coercive discipline = 16.59; F grade for fathers' coercive discipline = 35.73. F grade for mothers' induction = 18.82; F grade for fathers' induction = 17.14.
7. F sex for mothers' coercion = 68.61; F sex for fathers' coercion = 157.62.

8. Correlations of parental child abuse include:

	Positive Correlations			*Negative Correlations*	
	Mothers	*Fathers*		*Mothers*	*Fathers*
Conflict with authority	.416	.376			
Coercive parent			Nurturant parent		
Youth view	.371	.352	Parent view	.336	.274
Parent view	.357	.335	Youth view	.282	.260
Nagging parents					
Youth view		.327	Family closeness	.299	
Parent view	.284	.263			
Parent worry about			Age of parents	.252	.226
excessive punishment	.302	.293			
Authoritarian parents			Self-esteem	.236	.172
Youth view	.270	.257			
Youth worry about					
parent's drinking		.298			
sexual assault		.247			
body development		.239			

9. M.A. Straus (1974). "Leveling, Civility, and Violence in the Family," *Journal of Marriage and the Family* 36 (1974), pp. 13–30.

10. *Positive* correlations of spouse violence include:

	Mothers	*Fathers*
Spouse violence—partner	.264	.264
Family economic crises	.168	.142
Dissatisfaction with standard of living	.175	.114
Parental child abuse	.162	.167
Parental coercive discipline	.152	.183
Alcoholism in the family	.136	.085
Youth conflict with authority		.161

11. See, for example, the work of Diana Baumrind and Martin Hoffman.
12. Correlations tend to be in the .20 to .40 range. Preliminary factor analyses suggest that these four parenting styles load on a common factor.
13. Correlations tend to be in the .15 to .30 range.

Acknowledgments

The following people, by being supportive friends of Search Institute, also assisted in the production of this book.

James and Shelby Andress, Dan and Alice Anderson, Charles and Peggy Arnason, Paul and Lavonne Batalden, Allen and Andi Barnard, Neil and Glenna Bealka, John and Dorothy Benson, William Bolm, Donald and Nancy Bottemiller, Philip and Carolyn Brunelle, Terence and Marilyn Davern, Mr. and Mrs. Dale Delzer, Mary Ann and Darwin DeRosier, Barbara and Donald Diebold, George and Jenelle Dow, Mr. and Mrs. Chester Eggen, Vince and Cathy Eilers, Thelma Elfring, Mr. and Mrs. R. S. Engman, Joe and Kimberly Erickson, Mr. and Mrs. Patrick Fitzgerald, Raymond and Betty Ann Gardner, Ronald and Barbara Gauger, Sophia and Luthard Gjerde, Fern and Larry Gudmestad, Gustavus Adolphus College, Dr. and Mrs. Kristofer Hagen, Dr. and Mrs. Edward Hansen, Alden and Beverly Hanson, Janice and Charles Heinecke, Pat and Jeffrey Jerde, Clifford and Ruth Johnson, Donald and Barbara Johnson, Helen Johnson, Raymond and Ruth Johnson, Mr. and Mrs. Roy Johnson, Mr. and Mrs. Robert Keeley, John and Joanne Kendall, Mr. and Mrs. Jay Kershaw, Mrs. James Kottom, Margaret Kurak, Doris and Roland Larson, Edward and Patty Lindell, Sara Little, Norman and Helen Lorentzsen, Eleanore Luckey, Georgia and Raymond Lundquist, Carl and Miriam Manfred, Corinne and Allen Metcalf, Shirley Michel, Mr. and Mrs. William Nord, Walter and Karen Northrup, Howard and Doris O'Connell, Wilbert and Maxine Oman, Richard and Rose Palen, Howard and Vicki Pearson, Charles and Barbara Peterson, Wilma and Roger Peterson, Mr. and Mrs. Martin Quanbeck, Albert and Gretchen Quie, Carolyn Rask, Katherine Rouzer, Francis and Barbara Scholz, Mary Jo Schwab, Marilyn and Robert Skare, Joseph and Sandra Skach, George Spindt, Ab and Marge Strommen, James and Judy Strommen, Merton and Irene Strommen, Strommen and Associates, George and Jean Sverdrup, Jill and Robert Todd, Reginald and June Torrison, Robert Tufford and

Jane Dunn, George and Connie Weinman, Sybil and Thomas Wersell, Lyle and Dorothy Williams, Jane and Michael Wipf, C. Gilbert and Kathleen Wrenn, John and Gloria Ziegler.

Index

Abortion, moral judgment, 79–81, 168–170

Abstract reasoning, 23, 34–36; and religious doubt, 114, 117

Abuse, physical, 190–93, 197; violence between parents, 195

Academic achievement. *See* Achievement, academic

Achievement, academic: excessive pressure for, 197; parental pressure, 189–90; parent-child communications, 214; parents' concerns, 157, 160, 161. *See also* Achievement motivation

Achievement motivation, 33, 47–49, 59; and antisocial behavior, 132; and interest in school, 15, 228n.2; and parenting behaviors, 195; and prosocial behavior, 127; and sexual intercourse, 59

Adolescence, early, 3–4, 30–31; moral development, 77–78; sexual development, 20–21; social development, 33–62; worries of, 63–69

Adolescents, young: communication with parents, 212–17, 219–20; sources of help, 200, 218

Adult friends, as source of help, 200

Advice, parents as source, 28–29. *See also* Help, sources of

Affection, demonstration of, 182–85, 195, 196; help for parents, 206; and pressure for achievement, 189

African Methodist Episcopal Church, 6

Ageism, 107; and religious attitudes, 24

Aggression, 10, 131–34, 233n.4; and parenting behaviors, 195, 196; and television, 19; and videogames, 20

Alcoholism of parents: and spouse violence, 195, 236n.10; worries about, 65, 66

Alcohol use, 4, 10, 13, 28, 77, 143, 144–46, 153, 234 Ch.11n.4; and interest in school, 228n.2; moral judgments, 79–80, 169; parent-child communications, 214; parents' concerns, 160; and religious views, 24, 122, 123; and school climate perception, 17, 18; and sexual intercourse,

Alcohol use (*continued*)
230n.33; sources of help, 28, 200, 201, 202, 205; worries about, 64, 66

Alienation, 10, 33, 42–43, 61, 229n.11, 12, 14; and parenting behaviors, 195, 196

Altruistic values, 126–29, 208; decline in, 209

American Lutheran Church, 6

Analyses of Search Institute study, 225

Androgyny, 47

Anger: and love, 39; at parents, 61

Antisocial behavior, 131–41; help for parents, 205; and interest in school, 15, 228n.2; and religious views, 24, 122, 123; and restricting religion, 233n.14; and school climate perception, 18; and sexual intercourse, 59, 230n.33; and social alienation, 42–43, 229n.12

Appearance: values of, 89–99; worries about, 63 –67

Attitudes: parental influence, 171; positive, toward school, 15–17, 18; toward religious institutions, 22–24

Authoritarian control, 186–87, 195–96 ; and alienation, 43, 229n.14; and chemical use, 154; and child abuse, 193, 236n.8; and excessive pressure for achievement, 190; and prejudices, 108, 123, 232n.3

Autonomy, 36–39, 44, 59, 143, 229n.6; development of, 33; of parents, 165; and restricting religion, 123; values of, 89–99, 102

Baptist General Conference, 6

Beer drinking, moral judgments, 79–80, 169–70. *See also* Alcohol use

Behavior, and moral standards, 77, 81. *See also* Antisocial behavior

Beliefs: and behavior, 81; Christian, 114–17

Benson, P. L., *Religion on Capitol Hill: Myths and Realities*, 118

Bible, beliefs about, 116–17

Biological maturity, 45, 103

239